DISCOVERING THE POWER OF CEREMONY

By Teresa Brown

Ballinger Publishing
41 N. Jefferson Street, Suite 402
Pensacola, FL 32502
www.ballingerpublishing.com

Printed in the United States of America

Set in ITCCenturylightcondensed

First printing: October 2012

ISBN-978-0-7971103-2-0
ISBN-9-780979-110320

Ballinger Publishing
41 N. Jefferson Street, Suite 402
Pensacola, FL 32502
www.ballingerpublishing.com

Editors: Dechay Watts and Steven W. Bannow, PhD.
Cover design: Kassie McLean
Book design: Rita Laymon
Copyeditor: Dechay Watts

*For Aaron, Ethan and Wyatt
You have taught me more about love
than I ever imagined possible....*

TABLE OF CONTENTS

ACKNOWLEDGEMENTS

I am fortunate to be surrounded by creative and intelligent people, many of whom contributed to the creation of this book. First and foremost, I wish to extend my gratitude to the two people who most directly helped me to write this book, Dechay Watts and Steven W. Bannow, PhD. After Dechay and I returned from a vision quest four years ago, Dechay used her incredible writing skills to help me turn my vision into reality. From the moment we first discussed my story, we knew that ceremony had to be at its heart. Your talent and friendship, Dechay, helped me find my voice. Steven has sculpted the manuscript into life. Without your editing skills, support, and love, this book would not have been possible. You have championed me to the finish in a way that no one else could.

I would like to thank my son, Aaron Cohoon, who encouraged me to write this book and who helped me with many details when it seemed impossible for me to follow through. I also offer my sincere thanks to Christina Pfeuffer. You are my best friend, Chris, and you provided me with your love and support and the reminder that we have been practicing ceremony for forty-five years. I certainly cannot forget to acknowledge the Girls — Maureen, Robin, Libbie, Lanessa, Kali, Caroline, Meghan, Kim, Cornelia, Renee, Donna — for your continuous support of my work. It is truly our book.

And I thank all the people who have trusted me and have participated in ritual and ceremony with me. My prayer is that we help keep it all alive for the next seven generations.

AUTHORS BACKGROUND

Teresa Brown has practiced as an Intuitive Medium for twenty-five years. Mentored by her grandmothers, she integrates grassroots spirituality, with her intuitive ability as well as shamanic knowledge, learned from other teachers.

Teresa is a licensed ordained minister. She has worked with many psychologists, gaining a better understanding of the human psyche. She is often referred by psychologists and holistic health practitioners for her energetic clearing work and spiritual counseling. Teresa teaches workshops about Psychic Development, Understanding Dreams, Psychic Protection, and Acceptance of Divine Gifts. She also takes women to the wilderness on Vision Quests. For more information about workshops or private consultations, please visit www.teresabrown.net or www.myenergeticclearings.com.

INTRODUCTION

"We are all spiritual, whether we believe it or not."
~ Deepak Chopra

For thousands of years, prayer and ceremony have healed the sick, lifted the spirit, and released the soul. In the Western World, however, those wishing to find answers to life's most profound questions often choose to look outside themselves – emphasizing the ego. I believe there may be a time and place for such things, but I am certain that each of us can find answers and can realize peace and happiness within ourselves through simple ceremony.

For more than two decades, I have practiced as an Intuitive Medium. My work is an absolute joy. I have witnessed incredibly powerful, positive changes in many people with whom I have worked as they have learned to get in touch with their intuition and free themselves. I have witnessed many people find closure through their communication with loved ones who have crossed over. I have also had the opportunity to facilitate many past-life regressions.

More recently, energetic clearing has taken a more prominent position in my practice. I have discovered that truly wonderful dramatic life changes can occur for those who have the intention to release and to clear negative energies. And, over and over again, ceremony has been an enormously important component of the process.

No matter what intuitive activity I am asked to perform, I have been repeatedly blessed with opportunities to observe amazing positive permanent change in hundreds of individuals. Integrating prayer, shamanic practice, communication with spirit guides and those who have passed, and other spiritual techniques, I have seen people transformed—enabled to live their lives in a richer more fulfilling way.

While I have always known that I had powerful intuitive gifts and close connections with other times and other worlds, I have not always given my full professional attention to practicing as an Intuitive Medium. I had to be open to the possibility and ready to make the move when I knew – within my heart – that the time had come. I spent many years with my main focus on working in sales and earning a good living – for a long time as a single mom – supporting my son and myself. I did intuitive work during those years but more as an avocation than as a sole vocation as my practice is now. Like virtually all of the most important steps that we take in life, this one – to dedicate myself to helping others—could only come because I was open to it and because I listened to my heart. This book, which celebrates ceremony and the enormous potential for positive transformation through its practice, also comes from my heart. It would never have been written if I had not decided to surrender to my true calling in life.

So, yes, this book is about ceremony, but it is also a story – my story. Within these pages, you will learn how I came to accept and ultimately embrace who I am and who I have been. This book contains personal, sometimes painful accounts of my Earth Journey as a developing spiritual being as well as insights into many of the ceremonial practices that have helped me to grow and to find my way to a rich, full, and peaceful life.

It is my deepest hope that, through this little book, more people will come to understand that ceremony is a liberating and healing practice. Beyond the common uses of baptism, graduation, bah and bar mitzvahs, marriage, retirement, burial, and many others, ceremony can better a community, honor the Earth, and connect us to the cycle of life. The essence of ceremony, then, is quite basic: to heal the Self and to progress in life.

You will be amazed at the results of ceremony when you let the process come from heartfelt love and caring. Simple ceremony—with or without the presence of witnesses—can truly be life altering. All you need is yourSelf and your intention to feel peace, happiness, and connection to spirit. Anyone can perform the simple art of ceremony at any time.

According to universal law, whatever you project comes back to you. Consequently, I invite you to read this book with an open mind, with an open heart, and with the knowledge that the intention of any ceremony must be positive. Understand clearly that any ceremony or ritual with intent to cause harm or interference to another will cause these negative things to happen to you.

The examples of ceremony discussed in this book are actual effective practices that I have participated in and have witnessed. Please always avoid recreational substances or alcohol during any of these ceremonies. Stay sober and listen – carefully – to the words of Spirit. This I promise: You will never regret integrating the practice of ceremony into your life. I hope you will be able to develop your own helpful ceremonies based on guidance from this writing.

In peace, love, and harmony ... be Blessed.

Teresa Brown

HOW TO USE THIS BOOK

This is both my personal story and a self-help book. It is my hope that my accounts of how simple ceremony has enriched and improved my life and the lives of many others will be of interest and benefit to you as well. Toward that end, I suggest that you read this book from start to finish the first time. This will provide you with an overview of how some or all of the suggested ceremonies can become an integral part of your life. Then, after your first reading, please use the book as a guide to reference any ceremonies that resonate with you. I ask that you always be clear about your intention as you participate in any ceremony, and let your intention come from love.

Chapter 1

Embracing Personal Ceremony

"Be not the slave of your own past. Plunge into the sublime seas, dive deep and swim far, so you shall come back with self-respect, with new power, with an advanced experience that shall explain and overlook the old." – Ralph Waldo Emerson

If you asked me to tell you my deepest darkest secret, the one secret that I have so carefully hidden all my life, I would tell you that I remember being from another world. I have memories of a different planet and of a different species that are as clear as my memories of being here at home last Christmas with my family.

I feel so much profound love when I remember the planet. It was colorful but without trees. It was a place where we spoke silently to each other with our thoughts. It was a planet with beautiful music, which was created as the planet itself responded to our vocal sounds and instruments.

I remember great energy from this place. Telekinesis and teleportation from one location to another were common and almost taken for granted. We traveled all over the planet, easily flying from mountainous regions to desert like areas.

Large bodies of water refreshed and nourished us. We drank straight from the lakes and rivers without fear. To us, the water was sacred.

All of us were relatively slim, and our heights did vary somewhat but not as much as ours do on Earth. I was happy in my silvery skin with no hair. We wore simple suits similar to the color of our skin; we easily blended into the landscape when we needed to make ourselves invisible to intruders.

There was little illness in this place. In fact, we were able to avoid many illnesses because we realized that our thoughts directly affected our health and we channeled our thinking accordingly. Our healers were much like shamans as we understand them on Earth. They worked with the thoughts and energies of the sick as well as their physical symptoms.

We made up a vast community and within that community were smaller units, like families. We had technology, but it did not seem to interfere with our family units. The energy of technology was different than that on earth and did not interfere with our natural vibrations. We lived, worked, and played in peace on this wondrous planet we called home. We honored it in every respect.

I remember making an agreement to come to this Earth to share the love and energy from the place I once called home. I am not the only one. Many beings from other worlds are here to bring energy from their homelands to help this planet. They share what they can, when they can. And now is the time for me to share the lessons I have learned. Ceremony is the key.

The way I accepted this world of a past life was through ceremony, and I accept who I am now in the same way. Memories, whether of 2012 or 1550, can make a difference in your perception and experience. Whether your memories are from another world, the birth of a child, a wedding, or the loss of someone you love, ceremony can help you get in touch with these memories and integrate the experiences into your consciousness in a loving and beneficial way.

It is through our choices and evolution of spirit that huge differences occur in our lives and happen to the well being of our incredible planet. The power of simple ceremony has greatly helped me to accept and understand the gifts that I came into this world to share with others. Now in my fifties, I increasingly find living on planet Earth to be a joyous experience. My journey, however, has not always been easy.

Being from a small southern town, I did not have much exposure to reincarnation or the possibility of other worlds. I remember—at around the age of eight—talking with a friend on the way home from school about beings from other planets. We both agreed such life was natural and made perfect sense. I kept this memory in the back of my head as I grew up.

Accepting the gifts of who I am has been an amazing yet challenging adventure. I spent years resisting the truth of mySelf because of my ego; my ego fought my Self-actualization. A healthy ego is important in terms of well being and our journey in this world. When we allow it to control us, however, it can wreak havoc in our lives as it has on our planet.

I love this planet Earth. Our landscape is filled with natural wonders of indescribable beauty. From my past lives, I know that all planets do not possess such beauty. Earth's vast fertile areas, rugged terrains, and different life forms fill my heart. I have been blessed with loving relationships not only with people but also with birds, dogs, cats, and other non-human animals as well as an intimate relationship with the Earth herself. I consider myself very privileged to call this planet my home.

As human beings inhabiting the Earth, we must slow down enough to see the beauty in our friends' faces and hear the laughter coming from our children. We must make changes in our everyday lives to obtain happiness and to take care of this planet.

Our world is so fast paced. The demands on individuals continue to become greater at work as well as at home. We all must make an effort each day to slow down and become mindful of our activities. Otherwise, if we are not careful, we will find ourselves assimilated into someone else's dream or mold. The only way we can keep in touch with our personal power is to pull back—each day—into the quiet stillness of ourselves, into our center. This will facilitate the happiness and peace that are part of our natural birthright.

Every day I see young people walking around with cell phones and other devices occupying their ears and other sensory receptors. This inattention to their surroundings leads me to wonder how they will learn to recognize the beauty or potential danger that is around them. We, as mothers or grandmothers, fathers or friends, must be examples by showing our children the best future for our world through our presence. Simply being here and living deliberately is most important, yet it is the human capability that we most often ignore.

When you think about it, we are all different: different backgrounds, different memories, and different experiences. For example, math is not a mystery to some people who easily calculate equations and solve incredibly complicated mathematical problems with ease. This is not the case for me. I do not really understand an engineer's ability to transform numbers into functional tools. Likewise, when I talk to an engineer and others who are excellent in math, I find that they do not always understand my abilities to talk to spirits. These differences do not make either of us right or wrong—just different.

All of us do share something extraordinary: our humanity. And, in this, we have our own work to complete. I promise you that the one thing in your life you will never regret is your inner work. Your inner work of digging the well within yourself will bring to you the cool nourishing water of spirit, which will both free your spirit and sustain you. In this process you will find love overflowing and everlasting. It is from this place that we find true happiness and peace of mind. And, at the center of existence—for many of us—is God or Creator.

We may call God by different names but as long as we are in touch with our hearts and allow Divine energy to direct us in this dance of life, none of us are outsiders. The same God Force connects us all. Let us make our journey a sacred journey. There is great treasure within each of us; if we simply allow ourselves the opportunity to look, we will find it.

Integrating Prayer into Your Daily Life

"Therefore I say unto you, what things soever ye desire, when ye pray, believe that ye receive them, and ye shall have them." Mark 11:24

My birth on this planet came in a small southern town in the 1950s to a loving mother and father. My parents and grandparents had a strong faith in God, and prayer was taught to me before I could speak. Every night, my mother or father would pray with me beside my bed.

By the time I was a teenager, it had become apparent to me that I was not like my friends and the others around me. In addition to having a continuous memory of another world away from this one, I was able to talk with animals and often encountered spirits from the other side. The ego part of me struggled with this information because it meant that I was different and perhaps would not be understood or accepted. So, I stayed with the safe and accepted method of getting answers through prayer and learned great lessons from this practice.

My grandmothers helped me understand how to pray and to accept as natural my ability to communicate with spirits. Voices of angels can be heard, they told me, if we listen for the messages. In my grandmothers' love and teaching I felt safe; what they taught me came through love.

In prayer, we connect to Spirit through our higher Self. As we connect to Spirit, we allow ourSelves to open up to the Goodness of the universe. We allow ourSelves to accept ideas, healing, and love from the source that connects us with all living things. In that quiet space of prayer we are with God/Creator and our voices are heard. We surrender the ego to the higher power. We clear a path for healing, for answers, and for miracles to come our way.

When I was fifteen, the doctors discovered that my sixty-two-year-old grandmother had a blood clot on her brain. They were doubtful that she would survive surgery. They warned us that, even if she did survive the surgery, she would more than likely be left without speech or eyesight and possibly more.

I loved my grandmother so much that I got down on my knees and asked God to heal her. Many other relatives and friends also prayed for her with intensity. The moment we received the doctor's report after her surgery, I knew that prayer had worked. My grandmother came through the surgery with ease and without any brain damage. Her eyesight and speech and movement were fine and she lived to be a healthy eighty-two years old before passing quietly at home in her bed.

When we pray, we must ask for the highest good to come to any and all of those for whom we pray, including ourselves:

> *Creator of All Living Things, I give thanks for Your healing love for*
> *[my friend or my body].*
> *Let Your strength fill my spirit and Your light banish any darkness.*
> *Wrap me in Your loving arms and bless me with peaceful acceptance. I ask these things ... Under Grace and In Perfect Ways .... Amen*

Whether your prayer is to Jesus or Buddha, The Great Mystery, Kwon Yin, or Allah depends only upon your preference. You may call on God or Creator or The Great Mystery. Since I was brought up Christian, I have a great love for and feel very close to Jesus. Yet, I also love Buddha and embrace many things about Eastern philosophies as well as Native North American beliefs and some of the practices found among the cultures of Native South Americans. What resonates with your heart and feels good for you to practice is the right choice, as long as it comes from a foundation of love and kindness.

Many studies have been conducted on prayer and have proven that prayer is the most effective form of energy healing. Because we are not separate from God when we pray, we are surrendering our desire to Creator. This can have amazing results.

When you pray, let the words come from your heart and give thanks for all that you have. Your prayer may be as simple as a deep breath with loving words about your desires, followed by a big sigh. The most important thing is to create a space to honor the sacred journey we call life. Spirit works miracles in our lives and we must learn to ask for miracles.

When we pray, we energetically shift from the world of the ego to the world of Spirit. The more we practice a ritual (time, place, ceremony), the more we groove the path within to create that energetic vibration. As you create a repetitive ritual and prayer from the heart, you must be mindful. Prayers must come from the voice of the heart.

One way to practice daily prayer is to choose a book of poems or prayers and read one every day. Then, sit in silence for five minutes and reflect on the reading. Light a candle or stick of incense before your reading to acknowledge Spirit and to invite the Divine. Ask your heart what you can learn from its message and sit quietly. You will be astounded by the lessons that come your way. You can find messages from eagles, passing strangers, and books. And you may sense warnings from spirit guides as well as alerts to new opportunities and encouragement from Mother Nature by simply stopping to pray and listen.

Whether you light a candle or stick of incense or get on your knees to surrender, prayer to Creator (some say Mother, Father, or God) starts shifting your consciousness into a state of mind that allows your natural connection to link up to Source or Creator. As you shift, it should become your intention—and the universe knows this—to allow your heart to be filled with love. When you pray, "Not my will but Thine be done," you acknowledge a need to let go of your personal ego. You acknowledge a Divine design with infinite power to create and design something far better than even you have in mind:

> *Dear [Father, Mother, God...] I am safe and guided by Your love;*
> *Lift me into Your loving arms;*
> *Fill me with the courage and strength to speak my truth*
> *and to walk the path of love.*
> *Put me where I need to be; show me the way.*

If you are yearning to express gratitude, light a candle and say a prayer of thanks for the day, your life, and for all the good you experience. Sit quietly for five minutes and focus on nothing but your breath. Our requests are granted when we are in a state of gratitude and acceptance: "Ask and it shall be given."

Prayer can be used to gain guidance and answers for any aspect of life. If you are searching for prosperity, invite the spirit of prosperity to come into your life and repeat the Prayer of Jabez found in 1 Chronicles 4:10:

> *"Oh that you would bless me and enlarge my territory. Let your hand be with me and keep me from harm so that I will be free from pain."*
> *And, as the Bible says, God granted his request.*

The discipline of daily prayer and meditation brings the rich rewards of peace of mind, faith in a higher power, and surrendering burdens with an inner knowing that help is accessible in any situation. It is important that we approach prayer with gratitude because our energy and connection to Spirit is returned. If we approach Spirit feeling that we have more, more is returned to us.

Even if you are in great pain, you can give thanks that you can still hear the voices of loved ones or see the sun rise. Sometimes we must have strength because the sadness is so great, but through our deep feelings, we find our heart.

Children can benefit from practicing prayer as well. In fact, clients frequently ask me how to keep their children from losing touch with their sixth sense. I often suggest that they teach their children to pray. By helping children find a quiet space to listen to their own feelings and thoughts, we teach them to learn to use their internal compasses. By learning how to keep themselves from getting lost spiritually, they can find their way back to their internal guidance and overcome difficulties inherent in being human.

A child psychologist whom I greatly respect helped me develop the following activity involving prayer. It really helps children learn that they are not alone and reminds them to call upon their own angels and guides to help them and to shield them from harm.

> *"Okay, let's say a prayer to ask angels to fill this room and help keep you safe while you sleep. How many angels would you like to have in your room?"*
>
> *Encourage your child to answer in any number he or she chooses. My grandson loves this and sometimes he asks for seventeen angels one night or it may be two*

*thousand or any other number on another night.
"Twenty-six? Okay."*

*Then, say a prayer together. The child will have fun
being reassured by prayer, thinking of the angels, and
learning more about numbers.*

*Now continue: "Dear God, thank You for filling this
room with twenty-six of Your angels tonight to help watch
over [name of child] and let their love and Yours fill this
room and this house with so much light that we will all
know that You are here with us.*

Thank You for the sunshine and the trees.

*Thank You for giving us perfect health and lots of friends.
Bless all our family and friends with Your love and light."
Now send love to your child and ask: "Do you feel my love
for you?"*

Wait for your child to answer "yes."

Then ask: "Do you feel the angels' love?"

*After another "yes," tell your child to choose a prayer and
ask the angels to protect and keep him/her safe. Tell your
child that angels are good and they can be called on at
any time.*

I find that this is also a wonderful prayer process for adults who are
traumatized and frightened. After all, each of us is a child in some way
and, without a doubt, we are all children of Creator.

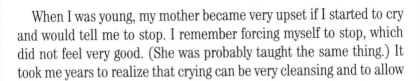

When I was young, my mother became very upset if I started to cry
and would tell me to stop. I remember forcing myself to stop, which
did not feel very good. (She was probably taught the same thing.) It
took me years to realize that crying can be very cleansing and to allow

myself to feel hurt and to feel sadness. I learned that our tears help heal our hearts.

Our world is full of joy and sadness, life and death, endings and beginnings. Emotions are a blessing that help us stay in touch with our feelings about these experiences. Crying is a perfect way to let go of the pain and sadness inside. Our tears wash away grief and sorrow concerning a multitude of things and they cleanse the heart.

Remind children that God is always with them and inside them. The simple exercise that follows can help your child learn to relax and calm himself. I taught it to my grandson with great success. At first, he was a bit hesitant, but now he uses it on his own whenever he wants to.

> *Say to your child: "Take a deep breath, deep ... Feel it in your tummy. Now let it out... That's good. Now take a deep breath again, slow, really slow.... That's it... .good.... All the way down to the tummy....Good, now let it out..."*

I encourage you simply to love and encourage children. Listen to them and their dreams, and have an open mind because they teach us as we help them. We receive the gift of guardianship to children when we become parents. Children come into this world with their own special gifts. As guardians, we are given the task to care for them and help them learn to grow into strong independent adults who will follow their true paths.

Meditation as Daily Practice

"Now for some heart work...." - Rainer Maria Rilke

Having memories of lives in a different world has its challenges. Many times throughout my life, I felt that I could not tell people what I know. When I was a teenager, a friend of my mother's looked at me and said:

"You are different, not from this planet." She told me that, in front of her eyes, I had changed into a different form and she was ... understandably, quite amazed. I knew in the deepest part of my being that it was true. But it definitely disturbed me to know that someone else could recognize this in me. What does a fourteen-year-old do with this type of information?

I decided to attempt meditation. I had read a couple books on Buddhism and thought that Samadhi would be a really good idea. I wanted immediate enlightenment and a way to understand how to leave my house without the fear of someone noticing that I was different. I remember thinking: "What if I go to a party and suddenly I turn into someone from outer space?!" When I think of this experience now, I am quite amused.

During my first attempt at meditation, I sat in my room staring at the wallpaper for what seemed like an eternity. Nothing happened. I had no idea of the patience required to get in touch with my center of being or with the blissful sanctuary to be found within. Being an impatient teenager, I gave up on meditation for a few years. I made a conscious decision to turn off everything: no more conversations beyond this world, no more thoughts of my past, no more being different—not even for just a little while.

This was denial in its purest form. I convinced myself that I had better not say too much about spirits or memories or somebody might get spooked and think that I was unbalanced. I learned the necessity of attempting to fit in early on as a result of an experience endured by the grandmother of a friend of mine. Sweet Grandmother Dora, whom I adored, was wonderful in every way and I wanted to be around her as much as I could.

There was a complication. Her family kept seeing her talk to birds. The birds would respond and come close to Dora. She also talked about spirits. Unfortunately, her narrow-minded son sent her to the state mental institution for several months because he thought she was insane. In order to survive, she changed her actions when she came home. No one saw her talking to birds again. How very, very sad, I thought.

My fears were understandable. I had a typical teenage ego combined with past life memories of people reacting unpleasantly to my spiritual gifts. Although I was fortunate to have very supportive parents and grandparents, my spiritual gifts made me feel different and I did not want to deal with them anymore. It took years and many vision quests for me to finally accept who I truly am.

My efforts to ignore the real me did not work out so well. I became a rebellious teenager who ran away from home. I got caught up in all the escapism of the '60s and became dependent upon drugs. I was miserable with myself as I lost touch with the spiritual girl who used to feel nothing but love for everyone.

My drug dependency landed me in a psychiatric ward, where I must admit I met some fascinating people. At the time, shock treatments were not uncommon and were used to "treat" certain psychological "disorders." Fortunately, I did not experience that form of treatment.

During my time in the ward, I made an important realization: All of the patients there, including me, perceived themselves as victims. This realization, combined with the fact that one of the nurses on call thought it was a good idea to take us all to see One Flew Over the Cuckoo's Nest, made me quit playing the victim. After two weeks in the facility, I carefully arranged an appointment with my psychiatrist and created a personal plan to be released.

You have to understand that the psychiatrist had a policy of seeing patients for only ten minutes at a time. At the ripe old age of nineteen, I knew that if I wanted to get out of that place I had to meet with him for almost an hour. I knew that I needed to tell him about some of my visions and why I got involved with drugs, continually explaining that my time on the ward had opened my eyes to the truth of the harm that goes along with drug use.

Honestly, only a fraction of what I told the man was true at the time. I was especially creative when I told him that my experience on the ward had made me realize how much I wanted to be a nurse! He loved that story and I was out of there within two days.

I tried to return home, but going back just did not work out. Fortunately, a very good friend invited me to come to live with her and her husband in North Carolina. She is the person who taught me to meditate and we are still close friends today—forty years later.

That time in the psychiatric ward was my first vision quest. It was a good initiation. I did not know about a rite of passage or vision quest ceremony, so life created one for me. I left my childhood behind and entered the adult world. I passed from girlhood to womanhood and, in that right of passage, I realized the world I lived in was not innocent— and neither was I.

I began a new life without drugs, cigarettes, alcohol, or meat and added plenty of exercise. Yoga and meditation became an incredible anchor for me and helped me realize that I could change my life. I learned that we can always go back to the basics; our energy can always rise and increase and it can always fall. The choice to increase our energy is up to us. Through it all, I practiced meditation, and it was through this practice of meditation that I realized where my heart center is.

———◆●◆———

One especially important kind of meditation is simply focusing on your breathing. Our breathing is one thing in life that we simply cannot live without. As we initially focus on breathing, we also become aware of the chatter in our mind. Through a practice of simply listening to our breathing, however, our mind eventually becomes quiet.

We can also meditate by visualizing a beautiful place in nature. As we silently go to this place, it becomes an inner sanctuary that we can access at any time. We create this place within and, as our mind becomes trained to be silent upon entering it, we open up to guidance from our intuitive realm. In the intuitive realm, we access our angels and our guides.

Meditation can be varied. Sometimes it can include chanting. Chanting has been used in many cultures for thousands of years. It is a wonderful way to open awareness, focus the mind on something other than thoughts, and access the inner sanctuary of peace. One can feel the resultantant resonance throughout the body. Try it and see how it makes you feel. When we chant, we are singing praises to Creator.

The first chant I experienced was this:
Om, Ma Ni, Pad Mi, Hum…
Om
Ma Ni, Pad Mi, Hum…
Om ….

I love different kinds of meditation. Sometimes I like to journey to my guides where I am able to ask questions and receive direction. You will be amazed at what advice and information guides can provide. All we have to do is listen and create the quiet space that is needed for the spirit guides to come through.

Meditation helps you to create the quiet space necessary to tap into incredible love and bliss within yourSelf. It does not matter your location or your living conditions. Your background makes no difference. With meditation, you have the capability to find peace and joy within your heart and the space to listen to your own counsel. Mother Teresa reminds us that, "Silence of the heart is necessary so you can hear God everywhere…"

We all lose track of our path at times and must practice listening to our own inner guidance. Once again, I think of the simple act of listening to our breathing. Simply learning to focus on your breathing is a wonderful way to start meditation as an exercise to tap into your inner peace and guidance. You can do this while sitting or when taking a morning walk. Whether you find a chant or a simple prayer that resonates as you pray, being mindful of your breathing will help your mind to become quieter until helpful inner voices or sensations can come through.

It is important that you try different things and stick to one or two for a while to become comfortable with meditation. Meditation CD's, podcasts, and music are just a few of the wonderful ways to incorporate a meditation practice into your daily life. You will be guided through your intuition and your desire to change and find that inner place of peace when it is time to change your meditation practice. You may be attracted to a yoga class, you may find a group to meditate with, or you may find that a new book with important insight simply falls off the shelf in front of you. But first, find a practice to help you focus on the silence within yourSelf. Within the silence, you will find peace, healing, and creativity. The ego steps aside while the heart and soul have an opportunity to be heard and there are voices from them that you may hear.

Ceremony 1.1: Focusing on Your Breathing

Sit in a space that feels sacred to you and focus on your breathing for twenty minutes. Let the ego or outer mind become quiet and listen to your inner voice. Feel your connection to Creator. Ask: "What is the most important message for me to learn today?" Do not try to create an answer. Simply focus on your breathing and let your thoughts flow freely.

Some people do not like to sit still to meditate. That's okay. You can take a walk in nature and observe the beauty of nature, trees, flowers, and birds while you listen to your steps and focus on your breathing. The more you pay attention, the more easily messages will come.

Ceremony 1.2: Giving Thanks

As soon as you wake up, walk outside and begin to count your blessings. Give thanks for your family. Give thanks for your friends. Give thanks for your body. Say a simple "thank you" to anything that you appreciate as it crosses your mind. Then, take a deep breath and feel the inner peace. Ask Creator to guide and protect you and show you the way. Listen and open your heart. This practice becomes your meditation. You must train your mind to be quiet.

Nature has an incredible way of surrounding us with her beauty and taking away all the frazzled energy of the day while she breathes fresh air not only into our bodies, but also into our very souls. I cannot help to think that the recent BP oil catastrophe in the Gulf of Mexico may have been prevented if the people in charge were taught as children that every creature has a family and a place in creation. If they had learned to take deep breaths to calm down and had been taught that the most important things in life are free, lives of working people may not have been lost and Mother Earth may not have been unnecessarily injured once again.

We have much to give thanks for in this beautiful world of natural resources and abundance. Yet our Earth is continually assaulted by lack of consciousness and greed. Only we can help by changing ourselves, connecting with Spirit, and guiding our children to have an awareness and respect for the environment. If we meditate in nature with Mother Earth, Gaia, she will help us understand how to help her. She is a living being.

Ceremony 1.3: Tree Energy

Go into your backyard or into a park. Lean against a tree and focus on your breathing.

Feel the tree's energy come through your body and notice how gently it carries any unrest into the earth…. now feel your body's energy change and become one with the tree's energy.

The spiritual energy of the tree neutralizes any negative energy and sends it into the earth, which leaves you feeling refreshed and positive. Place your palms onto the ground and lean over as close as you can and kiss the earth…or simply say: Thank you for letting me be alive! Thank you for my life!

We all need our egos. They take care of us personally and in the material world and they are necessary for a healthy life. But keeping the ego at bay is the practice that lets Spirit come through. We must learn to let the ego stand aside to personally develop and progress in a positive way.

We must listen, connect with our hearts, and trust the process. More than any other ritual, meditation will help you stay on the path, heal your heart, and keep you centered.

Through the practice of meditation, you build, inhabit, and expand your inner sanctuary of peace. Consider this: If you are mining for gold, there is virtually always much digging to be done at first—before you find your treasure. Inherent to the process is the need for patience. The same is true with meditation. You must remind yourself to sit quietly, breathe, and listen—patiently. When you reach the mother load of meditation—the ability to allow Spirit to come through—and you realize how much you have discovered in doing so, you will never be without again.

As I have mentioned previously, atmosphere can play a very important role in experiencing the greatest fulfillment from meditation. Creating a comfortable, fertile place for your own sanctuary at home can begin with a small, simple altar where you place statues—symbols of the deities you choose to call upon such as Jesus, Mother Mary, Buddha, Kwon Yin, and/or others.

Take some time each day to go to your sanctuary to honor and connect with this place in your outer world, which allows you to energetically call upon your deities for assistance. A good time to do this is just before meditation. This ceremony can help you to open up sacred space and help you shift from the world of the ego to the world of Spirit.

Prepare each day to unfold into your highest good by beginning with prayer, gratitude, and meditation. When you add positive affirmations into the mix and use the present tense for all that you desire, life will get better. Thoughts and speech are affirmations, so it is important to learn to communicate with loving kindness; both when you speak and in your thoughts to yourself.

Consider, for example the following affirmations to yourself:

> *I am loving and I am lovable; I now allow myself to be true to who I am this day!*
> *I am confident and beautiful, and I am in perfect health. I now allow myself to receive prosperity and use it for my good in every way!*

Another way to meditate is by journeying. In a journey, you enter a private and beautiful place that is created in the spirit world. You may enter a garden full of exotic plants, luxurious fountains, and peaceful places in which to lounge. You may find yourself in a quaint house in the woods next to a cozy fire in the bedroom of your dreams. You may wander down a dirt path into a jungle when you suddenly enter a clearing where all your guides appear. The inner worlds are rich with experience and joy. But, the Spirit world does not have a road map for us to follow. Allow yourself to be guided and, by following your own inner light, you will find the way to the answers you seek.

Sometimes a journey into your inner world will deliver immediate answers to your most pressing questions. Sometimes it will bring you to a place where you will simply ask questions. Know that the answers will always come when you are ready to hear them.

Answers can come from anywhere; a significant feeling may come to you about an issue or personal problem—at any time. This will lead to a new-found peace. A conversation in a restaurant that you overhear may contain your answer. A friend could call and say something that sparks you. The key is to be open and to remain open.

———————◆●◆———————

One day, I was driving to another state to work with a significant number of my clients. I was feeling sorry for myself because I was focusing on the huge load of upcoming medium work, which lay ahead of me. (Yes, even mediums can feel pressure and stress!)

Soon, I passed a huge billboard with a Bible verse, which basically said: "Wouldn't you rather be persecuted for good work than for evil doing?" Well the message was loud and clear. I got it!!! The pity party stopped as I continued driving toward my destination—somewhat embarrassed but back in focus. In touch with my purpose and my heart, I was capable, once again, to be helpful to each of my clients.

I promise you that if you begin and continue the practice of meditation each day, you will be thrilled at the joy and peace that you experience. You will begin to look forward to your meditation time. As you embrace a daily ritual of meditation, you create a space to receive the true power of Spirit. You will find that meditation is a way for you to center yourself and to find peace and guidance from your inner voice. You will find that you are the power in your world.

BLESSINGS

Creating the time to pray and meditate reinforces our intention to become as close as possible to our inner truth and happiness. Another way to continue to open your awareness is to say simple blessings throughout the day. Bless everything and everyone around you through positive words and thoughts to transform energy into heart-warming experiences. I truly believe that our loving thoughts can transform the world.

As Dr. Masaru Emoto suggests in his book, The Healing Power of Water, words of love are powerful. He explains how positive words and blessings can actually transform the food and water that we use in everyday life as well as the planet and all of its great bodies of water.

During the tragic time in Japan when the waters were filled with radioactive materials following the 2010 Tsunami catastrophe and consequential nuclear power plant damage, Dr. Emoto sought the help of each of us—no matter where we lived. He asked that we each go outside and pray at noon everyday. He asked that all of us tell the Spirit of the water that we were deeply sorry for the harm that we had caused it, and he asked that we tell the water's Spirit how much we love the water. I did what Dr. Emoto asked and added how profoundly sorry I was for the harm that we had caused the Gulf of Mexico waters.

As in a prayer, to be effective a blessing must come from the heart and be full of love and Spirit. A blessing is something that we bestow on someone or something like our food or our homes. Some blessings are meant to bestow holiness, such as those said at a child's christening or a couple's wedding ceremony. Anytime we open our heart to ask

Creator to come into a situation, to let our ego stand aside, and to form our intention with sincere thoughts and words, we can create a blessing.

Consider, for example, Thanksgiving dinner. This has always been one of my favorite meals because there seems to be extra time allowed to bless the food and one another. So many times, we rush through meals and miss out on conversation, forgetting to savor time with our family and friends, much less bless the food we are about to consume. Nevertheless, many of us in North America do find a time at Thanksgiving to bless our food and all that we have through prayer.

Blessing your food can be as simple as saying to yourself: "I am thankful for this food and for those who gathered and prepared this meal. I ask that this food be blessed with love and nourishment for my body. Amen."

Consider how American restaurant staffers often rush their customers in and out to encourage turnover and to put more money in their pockets. Gulping down food that is high in fat and low in nutrition and rushing through junk-food feeding frenzies is often the norm for their patrons. This does not have to be the case.

I love the much healthier attitude that many European cultures have toward eating. In the cafes that I have experienced in France and Italy, for example, the focus was on the occasion; there always seemed to be a sense of celebration surrounding the meal. Proprietors were keenly aware of this and made a conscious effort to be sure their patrons always felt welcomed, never rushed. In fact, people were often politely turned away when a restaurant was full to avoid groups of people hovering about. When we were able to share a meal at a restaurant, we were encouraged to take our time and to enjoy the blessings of nourishing food, engaging conversation, and wonderful friends. At home we have the choice of creating a healthy relaxed atmosphere for our families and ourselves during mealtime in a similar fashion.

Doesn't that sound like the best way to receive the best of everything important at mealtime?

Slow down and be conscious of the food you are about to take into your body. Think of the origin of the food and give thanks to the people and animals that helped make your meal truly a blessing. Our great need here is to slow down, to be mindful of what and how we eat, and to bless the food before we take it into our bodies as nourishment.

Another fantastic time to do a blessing is when you move into a new home or office. Blessing the space in which you will live or work is an age-old practice used by many cultures to cleanse and clear away any negative spirits or energy. You may feel stagnant energy or a bit uncomfortable in the new space, regardless of how much you love the way it looks. A simple clearing ceremony and blessing can produce amazing benefits.

A client of mine in Georgia needed a buyer for his beautiful condominium. It had been on the market for months and he needed to sell it quickly. When we went to the condo to cleanse and bless it, he found a note under the door from the condo association. The note related a very sad story. It disclosed that the previous tenant had leaped from the balcony of the building and committed suicide.

Keeping the note in mind, we went inside and cleansed the condo and blessed it with all things good. After the blessing, I went into the alley of the building. There I saw the spirit of the tenant who had jumped and I was able to speak with him. He expressed a great deal of sadness. We communicated for some time; he had much to relate. Eventually he was able to clear a way for himself to see his angel waiting for him ... to carry him to the other side. Three weeks later my client called. The condo had sold at his asking price!

There is much more to be said about clearing property but for now we will focus on how a simple blessing of any property can shift the energy and invite peace, harmony, and prosperity. When you do a blessing, remember that the power of intention is most important. It is essential to choose simple tools to assist you and ground the energy. A clearing ceremony and blessing can make the space feel much lighter after someone has been sick or any emotional upheaval has taken place in a home, office, apartment, or other living/working space. And, it only takes minutes. Anyone can do the following very simple yet effective ceremony.

Ceremony 1.4: Blessing a Space

Open a window or door to let out any negative energy that the blessing and cleanse might release. Pour sea salt into a saucer and hold the saucer in your left hand. Say a prayer and bless the salt with your right hand. (Example: I ask that this salt will be blessed with love and peace.) Next, go through the house/office and sprinkle a few grains of salt in every corner, in closets, under beds, behind furniture. Then, say a simple prayer to bless the space with positive energy. (Example: Creator, let this place be filled with love and peace; may only those who come in love enter here.)

Note that the salt in the previous ceremony neutralizes negative ions to give your space a general clearing. It is similar to the refreshing feeling you receive from swimming in salt water at the beach or taking a bath with Epsom salts. Please always remember to direct anything you clear into the light. It is our responsibility to ask only for the highest good for all.

A friend of mine who is a teacher in Texas used a cleansing ceremony to resolve an issue with a disruptive child in her classroom. She had tried many things to work with the child to no avail. After school one day, she opened the door slightly, blessed and lit some sage, and said a prayer to clear her classroom of negative energy. She was amazed at how quickly things changed. Within days, the disruptive child was transferred to another classroom! Attitudes among the other students quickly improved and she was able to teach her class with relative ease.

On a different occasion, one of my clients in North Carolina called me because her eight-year-old grandson had been having night terrors for months. He would continually wake up screaming about something in the closet. (Sometimes children become frightened because they are much more sensitive than adults and tend to see, hear, or feel pesky entities in their bedrooms. At other times, they may have seen or heard something frightening on television or actually experienced something that made them upset.)

In this case, I was assisting my client remotely by phone and advised her to clear her house. When everyone else had left the house, she opened a window in the boy's room. She used sage that she had blessed throughout the house, opening the closets, and noting the change in energy. Later that evening we had a follow-up phone conversation during which we both focused on clearing any negative energy from the home. I used a clearing technique to help direct the energy and we said a prayer and blessed the house and her grandson's room with love. Five months later, she called and told me that her grandson had not woken up with a night terror—not even one time—since that ceremony.

I highly recommend that you try the simple, age-old practice of cleansing and clearing to bless your space. You can even bless your vehicle, a shed, or a hotel room when you check in. You may use any of these techniques or combine them. Remember it is your intention that is most important. And always remember that the power within you comes from Creator. Creator's power flowing through you is the energy that clears your space. It is your faith and intention that allows this to happen. You are as capable as anyone to perform these blessings and clear your space.

As you begin to bless everything around you and incorporate ceremony into your daily life, you will feel more connected and alive. People, earth, and animals will take on intriguing vitality as you feel their Spirit. You will come to see the magnificent natural wonders of the wilderness and the oceans and be in awe of Mother Earth's provisions.

It is up to each of us to incorporate this awareness into our actions by respecting, honoring, and blessing Mother Earth and all that she cares for. She provides a home for us and takes care of us—generation after generation. Through blessings, we can return a small part of the care and nurturing dedication Mother Earth provides.

Ceremony #1.5 (A Blessing for our Great Mother Earth, Gaia)

Go outside in a quiet area and sprinkle an herb like sage or sweet grass on the ground. (You can generally find these herbs at a natural health food store). Get down on your knees and place your hands on the earth. Give thanks to Our Great Mother Earth, Gaia, for your life. Bless her with your love and kindness. She will return the thanks that you give with her own blessings for you.

Native Americans tell us that our inner work is passed on for seven generations. Taking the time to appreciate Mother Earth, learn from her, and teach our children to respect her will only help us in the future. After all, where would we be without her love?

Turn off your phone and the television and turn off your computer. Then listen to your surroundings, to your heart, and to the voice within yourSelf that longs to be heard. We are all part of the great circle of life; we are not here to rule over or dominate others. There is plenty of opportunity for us to change but we start at home, in our bodies, in our lives—by listening.

———————◆●◆———————

As we cultivate our inner sanctuary through prayer and meditation, these rituals coming from the heart create a natural shield of protection. This protection comes from Spirit. Spirit is the essence of creation, our link to Source, which connects us to all living things. The more we are connected to Source, the more love, joy, and happiness we experience. You learn to trust in that Spirit within yourself—the small voice within—by taking the time each day to listen. Some days you may feel as though you hear very little, but there are days when you will sit in the rushing silence in complete awe of a river of love flowing through your own heart.

Meditate and/or bless or pray in faith that you are not alone. Have faith that you will connect to Source. Then hope your prayers will be answered. In the silence rushing through, you will feel love. We know that the love is from a Source far greater than we can imagine and that love connects us to everything that lives on the Earth and beyond the galaxies. We cannot abide in this place of Source indefinitely or we would be enlightened and in another dimension. But our human experience gives us the opportunity to connect to this great love and diverse experience.

As you create personal rituals to help you connect to Source, to Creator, please remember the essence of 1 Corinthians 13:13: Three things will last forever—Faith, Hope, Love—and the greatest of these is Love.

Chapter 2

Developing Community & Finding Your Heart

"Listen and intend with the ear of your heart." - Saint Benedict

As mentioned in the last chapter, daily ceremony creates a relationship between you and the Spirit world to bring clarity and peace into your life. It will become comfortable and fruitful to practice daily ceremony alone as a secret ritual in your private sanctuary. Later, you will discern the power of sharing that incredible connection to Spirit in a circle of truth with friends, family, and perhaps even like-minded strangers in your community.

More than a decade ago, I joined a group formed by a spiritual and creative psychotherapist. We met in a circle each week and spoke from the heart about matters of life, love, and spirit. During these gatherings, I witnessed great healing and heartfelt expressions. At times there were tears, but the tears became a pool of acceptance, healing, and love, which was void of painful emotional attachment.

I came to this circle with a broken heart, after a painful divorce. I struggled to find peace within mySelf and to gain understanding about how I could possibly begin a new life. I had lost so much. In the sacred space of the group circle, I found the freedom to speak openly about my feelings in front of more than one person for the first time in my adult life.

Growing up, I was encouraged to keep quiet about many things and learned to "stuff" my feelings. I know I am not alone. It is sad to admit that I seldom meet people who have had consistently healthy inter family communications. All too often, parents do not understand how to communicate, and they teach their children to hold back on expressing feelings of anger or hurt in the same way that they were taught to hold back their own feelings.

As we mature, we have an opportunity to unravel that confusion. Gathering in a circle creates a space for clarity and love to prevail. Because we cannot open our hearts to everyone, sacred circles allow us to open our hearts safely in a group situation where we promise to keep everything that is spoken within the circle. Nothing leaves the circle in which we speak.

The sacred circle is not a new phenomenon. The circle represents infinity with no ending or beginning. The circular shape of the birth canal or of the sun or moon is considered a sacred shape in most cultures. In the ancient ruins of the Anasazi people in the southwest region of what is now the United States, archaeologists found rounded spaces known as kivas both in cliff dwellings and flat areas. These circular areas were used for spiritual ceremonies thousands of years ago.

Many Native Americans believe that entering a circle formed by their community must be treated with the same respect as when Christians enter a church. They use the sacred space for celebration, dance, and healing and sit in circles for ceremony and to discuss matters of importance. Some indigenous people have separate women's or men's circles, using specific ritual or direction of movement depending on the gender.

People may gather to express reverence, to speak their truth, or to gain guidance for the community. Fire is often used as the centerpiece of circle. Music, drums, and dance may also be part of the ceremony to express joy and communicate feelings.

Consider what your life would be like without the interference of electricity or technology. Without modern day distractions, you could focus on the elements of life that you enjoy and love the most. What speaks to your heart? Watching the sunset at the beach? Being held in the arms of your beloved? An early morning walk as the birds and world awaken? The simple pleasure of laughing and playing with your child or grandchild? The joy of these activities is timeless. To sit in a circle where you learn to speak from the heart and know that you will be listened to attentively, without judgment, is also timeless. The beauty in this timelessness is that we can take part in it now as easily as our ancestors did five thousand years ago.

In our modern society, it is easy to lose touch with our roots. Through the process of becoming assimilated into a fast-paced, ego-driven society, we lose sight of many valuable lessons. We seldom sit quietly with ourselves or with others. Seeking the help of a qualified counselor can help resolve issues, but often we simply need a sacred space to speak without inhibition or fear of judgment. Ancient practices like sacred circle can build loving bonds that improve our personal lives and communities.

It is truly amazing to be part of a circle that meets on a regular basis. You will find yourself looking forward to this time of opening the heart. As you repeat the process of the circle, you begin to recognize the difference between words from the heart and words from the head or ego. Often, people rediscover expressions from the heart that have been well hidden for years. It is a place where ego melts away and you begin to see the pure light that resides inside each and every one of us. It is a space where true friendships are born.

Through a circle formed with just a few friends, you can positively affect the lives of many. In my own life, the circle gave me hope and inspiration. It was in the circle that I was finally able to express feelings of great sorrow about my divorce. It was here that I began to speak of other-world memories and learn that those present recognized that part of me and were perfectly fine with it. I dug deeper into my own path of Self-acceptance. I was able to find my heart again. I cannot overstate the importance of this. Without heart, our world becomes cold because we are disconnected from Source. But with heart, we live and speak our truth and learn to love ourselves, others, and the world we live in. From our hearts, doors to realms we never dreamed were possible open for us.

I have witnessed incredible healing during the many circles that I have shared. In one circle, a man who was adopted shared his newly-realized understanding of why he had such a tremendous need to control and organize his life. In another group, a woman tearfully spoke of her child being molested. Amazingly, five other women in the circle shared how they had been molested as children. Three of the women had never shared the experience with anyone. These women felt that healing took place for them simply because they could express this horror and know that they were loved and accepted just the same. In still other circles, I have seen people recognize life-long dreams and their desire to pursue them, knowing that they deserved the good these dreams would bring.

Circle provides space for people to express their deepest feelings. As you listen, you remember that you are not alone in what you feel and find that answers often come as others express their thoughts. When we feel safe enough to be honest and speak only from our hearts, healing takes place. Circle becomes an incredible experience in an environment where the basis is unconditional love.

Circles give birth to new spiritual communities, which can grow and spiral into other circles to extend the community. These new communities bear no obligations, yet they have a strong foundation, which we can always return to whether we meet with some or all of the community members.

Consider this: Each day we all walk upon the same earth, whether our steps fall here in America, or in Africa, or in China, or anywhere else. Our skin may vary in color but it still functions in exactly the same way—covering our human bodies. We share oxygen, which is created by plants all over this beautiful Earth. Our energy comes from Source; it is this same energy from Creator that creates and connects us all. We all share warmth and energy from the same sun. The same moon affects tides on the Gulf Coast of Florida as well as the Cape of Good Hope, the North Sea, or the Pacific Ocean. We are one and when we connect with this oneness within us we recognize that there is no separation or pyramid. It is the ego that attempts to convince us one is more important than another. The truth is death makes us equal. So why not recognize equality now? Each of us is part of the great circle of life. No one being is any more or less important than any other.

The circle can help you carry your feelings of oneness into experience with others in a safe and positive way. When the collective mind has positive intent, great possibilities are available. Circle creates a foundation for more strength with the courage to change. It is a time when you are never alone and are always loved by the spirit who walks with you and those in your community whom you have learned to trust.

The circle has become a cherished way for me to experience true community. As I encounter members from time to time, a knowing smile will pass between us. An unbroken bond of the spirit connects us through trust.

Circle creates loving relationships over time. You can feel the love wash over you like a gentle wave on the shore in the early morning sun. Allowing ourselves the opportunity to speak from the heart and listen without judgment from the ears of the heart can be life- altering. This practice leads to renewal, and there is no limit to the healing that can take place in our own lives as well as in our world.

We can take the love and non-judgmental attitude that we generate in circle with us to work. We can take it home to our families and use it to listen with a new ear. How our world can change! As circles continue to spiral outward, untold miracles will surely occur. It simply starts with you, with your willingness to change, to speak your truth, and to be true to your heart.

Sometimes the heart wishes to speak what our egos do not expect. We cannot open our hearts to everyone we meet since some people do not have our best intentions in mind. It is imperative that we create space to nurture relationships that are built on trust and acceptance. By listening to our hidden voices and those of our community, we give ourselves a chance to transform our lives and become free.

I encourage you to take a few minutes each day for meditation. Listen to the quiet within, get to know your guides and deepest feelings, and step forward with your family or a few friends and form your own circle. There is no better way to create strong bonds of the heart inherent in sacred circle.

Ceremony 2.1: Ceremony for Creating a Circle of Truth, a Sacred Circle

Have your group sit in a circle. You can sit on the floor, on pillows, or on chairs.

Avoid chatting. Soft music can be playing in the background if you wish. You can also begin by drumming for a few minutes to shift the energy. Sage is often used for clearing a space; it helps clear our energetic fields by simply moving the smoking herb around our bodies—a process referred to as smudging.

Agree that nothing spoken in the space or room leaves the Sacred Circle.

Choose an item to be used as a talking staff. In some Native North American tribes a feather is used for the staff. You can use a feather, a staff made of wood with ornaments or beads, or you can use a simple rock or shell.

(On a personal note, I have found that circle can be an incredibly sacred space allowing us to create truly deep connections with others. Before embarking on one of my first vision quests, my mentor made a point of emphasizing the importance of circle. In fact, he asked me to find an object that I could one day use as a talking staff. Soon after, I found what I was looking for: a heart-shaped rock the size of a fist. It was representative of my own heart during this important early vision quest and became the talking staff that I have often offered for use during many of the circles I have participated in since.)

The speaker holds the talking staff as he or she speaks from the heart. No one else should speak during this time. If you feel compelled to respond to the speaker, reach for the talking staff and hold it before speaking aloud.

The talking staff is slowly passed around Sacred Circle. If you do not wish to speak when the talking staff comes to you, you may simply pass it along.

When it becomes your turn to hold the talking staff and speak, introduce yourself with your given first name or a spirit name. It can be a name that you choose to share at the time.

Remember this is a place of heart and soul, not of the ego. Your first or last names do not matter. Neither does your profession or job title. You are here in circle for other reasons. Native Americans teach us to speak and listen with the heart.

When the staff is passed your way, hold it and wait. Listen closely. You will learn to recognize the difference between the voice of the head or ego and the voice of the heart.

Everyone present listens with the heart. No one says anything or responds unless they feel moved to speak. If they do wish to speak, they should reach for the talking staff or place their hand on the staff while speaking. This is a powerful way to let people know they are heard and to teach the person who responds the importance of responding from the heart.

There is never any pressure or judgment during circle. When a person with the staff speaks, and someone feels compelled to respond, they simply reach for the staff and hold it while responding. What is most important in sacred circle is that each person in circle has an opportunity to be heard with unconditional love and without judgment.

After meeting several times with your circle, it becomes easier to feel your true voice come through. Words from the heart flow easily and often reveal deep pain that has not been shared or great dreams that have yet to be lived. You will begin to realize that your truth is your power and it has a voice of its own—a voice to be respected. The added support and love from a trusted group can only heighten self-acceptance as it creates community strength.

Imagine what changes would take place if our schools held sacred circle every week in the classrooms or Senate members could only speak while holding a talking staff during their sessions. Imagine the difference when truth and love prevail in our lives. It can only bring us more awareness of the importance of respect for ourSelves and for others. Learning to let our ego stand aside while our hearts and the hearts of others speak in kindness of true feelings and dreams can unleash limitless potential for Good.

In order to improve our world, we must mindfully practice our own truths. We must be willing to change personally and speak from our hearts. You cannot open your heart to everyone, but having a few core people who believe in you and love you without condition makes all the difference. Start where you are and open up to the possibilities of creating your own Sacred Circle, both in the privacy of your home as well as in a communal space. Limitless possibilities are created when even only a few people come together and allow truth to expand.

DRUM CIRCLES

In 1991, during testimony before the United States Senate Special Committee on Aging, Grateful Dead drummer, Mickey Hart, stated:

> *Typically, people gather to drum in drum circles with others from the surrounding community. The drum circle offers equality because there is no head or tail. It includes people of all ages. The main objective is to share rhythm and get in tune with each other and themselves. To form a group consciousness. To entrain and resonate. By*

entrainment, I mean that a new voice, a collective voice, emerges from the group as they drum together.

As Mickey suggests, another powerful way to gather in community is to form a drum circle. Your group is sure to have fun and, while doing so, tune in and connect with each other. A drum circle can be an exciting way to open up and shift consciousness from the world of the ego to sacred space or it can stand alone as a voice emerges from the community of drummers.

If you have ever drummed with a group, you know how excitement increases during the time you are playing. A clear, collective voice emerges; it is the voice of the drumbeat. You do not have to have any experience drumming to participate. Simply play as a child would play and enjoy yourself while your rhythm emerges.

Years ago, I attended a drumming workshop which was taught by a therapist who was in a wheel chair. As he taught us some simple techniques for drumming, we gained confidence in our drumming ability. He shared with us stories of his drumming instruction to troubled boys. He told us how drumming led them to bond with each other and to gain self-confidence. Eventually, they were able to travel to other schools to perform. Through the drumming group, each boy's self esteem became much healthier. It's amazing that such positive changes took place in the boys through the collective voice of his group!

While drumming groups may gather for Solstice Ceremony or other major celebrations, others may simply gather for recreational music and supportive community. In our fast-paced society and its craving for instant gratification, we seldom sit without constant, distracting chatter—from ourselves or from others—much less take time to speak from the heart. The freedom to speak and be heard in a sacred space without inhibition or judgment builds loving bonds that improve our personal lives and work relationships and can be perpetuated throughout our communities.

Speaking our true feelings from our heart brings peace and newness. Whether we are sharing joy, great sadness, or a special dream or discovery we may have made, it is important to our sense of well being that we have people in our lives whom we trust and count on to share what we wish to express. Our heart speaks and the soul rejoices.

"In the church of my heart, the choir is on fire." ~ Mayakovsky

Chapter 3

Honoring Your Body With Movement

"The strongest, surest way to the soul is through the flesh." ~ Mabel Dodge

It is an-early April Saturday morning. I sit inside my tent listening … to the drizzling rain and the sound of surf murmuring in the background. My body aches from yesterday's hike to reach our wilderness campsites. We brought in our packs and our water, and our trek seemed to take hours. We will be here—on our wilderness fast/our quest for two days before hiking back to civilization.

We fasted all day yesterday, which made the day seem so much longer. I slept for almost twelve hours last night and —having had nothing except water today—I am hungry. I feel good as I contemplate the moment and the resilience of the amazing human body.

The body houses our brain, our heart, our lungs, and all of the other utterly astounding tissue-parts that we need to efficiently carry us through our journey on earth. The Celts call the body our clay home, and it needs to be nourished, cared for, and honored. Without it, we are no longer physically present in this world. When our clay home is in distress—often due to lack of proper care—we become distracted and/or ill. Late tonight I will sit out under the stars by a campfire, enjoying the privilege of being human and the magnificence of Nature in all her glory.

My mind changes its focus to the new energy that is generated when we detoxify our bodies by fasting—as I am doing now. In my contemplation, I am reminded of a walking meditation used to stretch the legs, relieve tension, and train the mind to be quiet to facilitate listening to the inner voice.

Ceremony 3.1: Connecting With Mother Earth (A walking meditation)

Stand up straight and tall while imagining a cord reaching from your center of gravity (located within your solar plexus area) to deep into the center of the earth. As you walk, be mindful of your body and notice how easily you move with grace and good posture. Be mindful of your breathing—deep from the belly—as you are connected to Mother Earth.

Breathe in and say/think:
I love my body;
Breathe out and say/think:
I Love the Earth.
Breathe in and say/think:
I smile to my body;
Breathe out and say/think:
I smile to the Earth.

As you walk, you may choose to repeat the same phrases or you may mention any part of the body in your phrase so that you lovingly pay attention to various parts of your body. As you do this, you are being mindful of what a joy it is to be present in your body.

Breathe in and say/think:
I smile to my heart;
Breathe out and say/think:
I smile to the Earth.
Breathe in and say/think:
I love the Earth;
Breathe out and say/think:
Creator, has Blessed the Earth.

As you focus upon your mantra and breathe, your mind becomes quiet, and you will find your Self feeling energized by how grateful you are to be present in your body while connected to the Earth.

Simply by walking daily and increasing the length of the walks, people have lost weight, lowered blood pressure and cholesterol, and improved overall health—mental and physical. Our bodies long for movement; we must allow ourselves the freedom of healthy movement. This all can begin with a simple daily twenty-minute walk.

In the latter part of last year, I went to Canyon De Chelly to participate in a ceremony to bless the Earth and to attend workshops. We camped on Navajo land. The scenery was spectacular. The most moving and inspirational part of my trip, however, was my meeting an incredible seventy-three-year-old Navajo guide.

As our group approached the canyon, I was surprised and more than a little apprehensive by the height of the walls we were told we would need to descend to reach our campsites. Being from Florida, with it much flatter landscapes and low altitude, I could not help my increasing fear of scaling down the canyon walls. Knowing that I had recently been neglecting my physical conditioning program and all too aware of the weakening of my stamina certainly contributed to my apprehension.

Nevertheless, down we went. After a while, I hesitated on a steep wall that I had struggled to climb down. As I stopped to catch my breath, a vibrant woman almost twenty years my senior literally skipped up the walls and asked if I needed her help. That was an awakening moment/an epiphany, really, for me. I later asked to take her photograph and, after doing so, told her that she was my inspiration for a rekindled dedication to getting into better shape. I promised to tell my friends of her, and she laughed heartily at my candor. Later, she told me that she previously did guide work almost every day, but lately she had not had as much opportunity.

I returned from my trip with many new insights but none as important as my renewed awareness of the need for daily aerobic activity. I had allowed myself to become much too comfortable with a minimal exercise routine, but now I was ready to rejuvenate my clay home through movement.

It is a shame that our contemporary American culture has neglected the importance of feeding the need for natural movement that our bodies crave. The Navajo woman who had inspired me had learned the importance of staying in excellent physical condition when she was a young child. And this lesson had become an essential part of her life. She told us how she would climb the steep walls each to catch the school bus and how she would climb back down again to return home at the end of the day. Being in shape had become natural to her. She is a perfect example of how regular exercise is vital to our physical and mental well-being. We must make the extra effort—for ourSelves—since most of us do not tend crops or climb canyon walls every day.

When I was in my thirties, my father passed away from a heart attack. Years of smoking lack of exercise, and diabetes had caught up with him. I felt that I had lost my best friend. We had been very close all my life and he was the person who taught me about unconditional love.

At the time of my father's death, I was married with a young child and had no formal fitness routine. I was slim and very busy with my family, but was not devoting time to conditioning through healthy movement. My motivation to get back into shape came to me when—shortly after my father passed away—I started having heart palpitations. The experience was terrifying, and the more frightened I became the more irregular my heartbeat became.

I went to a heart specialist who told me that I have a prolapsed mitral valve. The doctor explained that the condition could cause me to feel dizzy and even to pass out. He said he could give me medication to slow the heartbeat down but the very best thing for me to do was to exercise. I became committed to daily exercise and joined an aerobics class, which seemed more like gymnastics to me. The class was helpful but I wanted more, so I became a certified aerobics instructor and started my own aerobics class. I enjoyed every minute of it and reaped the benefits.

My intuition was correct: I had concluded that my body was in need of exercise, of healthy movement—not pills—to naturally regulate itself.

For seven years I taught step aerobics, low-impact aerobics, and a special seniors aerobics class at a local medical center. Witnessing the significant improvement in myself and in my students was energizing and inspirational. Our time together was a joy in so many ways: We enjoyed the music; we laughed; we had fun; we became much more healthy. The classes were designed for anyone who wanted a good workout. The seniors learned to monitor their blood pressure and cholesterol on a regular basis. The results were lower blood pressure, lower cholesterol, and increased lung capacity.

After a few months of low-impact aerobics, we added a belly dance class. Many of the participants made gorgeous costumes, which only added to the fun. One of my more introverted students (we'll call her Betty), who had been a caregiver for her bedridden husband for two years, came out of her shell during the belly dance class.

We all teased and bantered with her. She began to wear make up for the first time in ages, laughed, carried herself beautifully, and totally enjoyed herself. We were all thrilled to see the positive change in her—physically and mentally. Betty had needed to feel more beautiful, more alive, and physicality helped to facilitate her amazing metamorphosis.

Life is certainly never easy but we all take action—even little things—to make ourselves feel better ... just like Betty did. The benefits of feeling younger—naturally—can only help us both mentally and physically and, consequently, improve the richness of and joy in our lives.

———◆●◆———

Aerobic exercise increases and improves circulation—the movement of oxygen through the blood in the body. Walking, swimming, and bicycling are examples of aerobic exercise. One need not be a gymnast or accomplished athlete to enjoy the benefits of an aerobic workout. Simply turn on some music and enjoy yourself while nourishing your health/your clay home by moving to the music. Or you may want to have an aerobic ceremony—incorporating our connection to the Earth with a group of people around a fire.

Ceremony 3.2: Circle Dance
This is an honoring celebration and can be used to honor a birth or

any other event deserving special recognition. It is a wonderful way to honor and bless mother Earth.

> *The group stands in a circle around a fire. Each person imagines a cord from the solar plexus to the center of the earth. You may choose to have a drummer or drummers creating a beat for all to step to as they circle around the fire. You may agree on a song or chant and move your arms and hands free form or simply move while placing your hands on your hips.*

Ceremony 3.3 Solstice Dance

The solstice has been celebrated for thousands of years. You can create your own very special solstice celebration in a backyard, in a wilderness area, or (my favorite) at the beach.

Drumming is always great addition to a solstice celebration. Drummers can sit in any area near the space where the ceremony participants step in and move or dance in a circle.

> *You may begin with a prayer or by calling in the directions —asking for blessings for the space and all the people assembled. Burning cedar or sage in the area is always helpful. The smoking sage and/or cedar may be passed to all of the participants.*

> *Let the drumming begin. As people start to dance, they enter their chosen space and move in the manner that they choose. The dance can go on for hours. The participants should be encouraged to sing, shout, chant, or howl. It is a time for celebration. The memories deep*

within will come back to life—as this is not the first solstice you have celebrated.

Honoring our bodies with movement is really about the basics of allowing or encouraging our bodies to do what they were intended to do. We can create ways in our daily routine to walk more, to take the stairs whenever possible, and, by all means, to find a way to regularly stretch our muscles. When the dogs that honor my home with their presence and companionship awaken, I love watching them stretch. They take the time to stop and extend their bodies into the position, which, in yoga terms, is the downward dog position.

Yoga is much more than exercise or stretching. Yoga is a way of life, a practice, a philosophy. Yoga has been very helpful to me throughout my adult life. As I mentioned earlier, yoga was a very important part of healing myself from drug and cigarette dependency during my early twenties. By practicing yoga daily—a routine lasting up to forty-five minutes—I found the peace and calm within mySelf and lost all desire for those toxic habits.

There are many kinds of yoga that are helpful for all ages. It is important that you are with a group or choose a style that is enjoyable and comfortable for you. Yoga should never be painful. It allows our bodies the opportunity to stretch gradually, and it helps us attain or regain flexibility, which is very important to our health. Warming up or stretching helps protect us from sprain, strain, and injury. I have observed women gain confidence in their bodies with simple concentrated stretches. Those of us who practice yoga and incorporate daily stretching moves routinely appear to be and, in fact, are more relaxed and able to take in more of the joy of life.

Ceremony 3.4 Gratitude with Extended Child's Pose

Light a single candle and place it on the floor near but not too close to a mat or rug upon which to kneel and stretch. Take a moment to give thanks to Creator for your life and body/the clay home that carries you through this world.

Kneel on the floor. Start with your knees a few inches apart. As you slowly lean forward, reach your arms forward with your palms outstretched. Steadily and slowly bring your palms and forehead to the floor. Simply remain in that position and feel the stretch.

With your forehead on the floor, be mindful again of your grounding into the Earth. During this simple and joyous stretch, be mindful of your body while the candle burns.

Take some deep breaths and (again) give thanks.

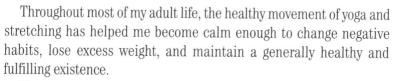

Throughout most of my adult life, the healthy movement of yoga and stretching has helped me become calm enough to change negative habits, lose excess weight, and maintain a generally healthy and fulfilling existence.

There are many personal ceremonies—other than those associated with yoga and stretching—that utilize movement. One of my favorite movement ceremonies is walking the labyrinth—a practice that has been used for thousands of years in many different cultures. The oldest labyrinth is in Crete, and it dates back more than five thousand years.

According to Greek mythology, the first labyrinth was the maze built to trap the Minotaur, a creature that was half man and half bull. It was a menace and needed to be dealt with. Eventually, the Athenian hero Theseus killed the Minotaur with aid from the lovely Adriane. She provided him with a skein of thread before he entered the labyrinth where the Minotaur resided. The skein provided the clew or "clue," he used to find his way out of the labyrinth after having fought and killed the Minotaur.

Labyrinths are found in many different areas throughout the world. Some are located in front of churches and are often made with paver stones. There can also be meandering walled pathways enclosed by hedges, stone, or—as created by a friend of mine —lovely seaweed and driftwood mazes. My friend periodically invites people to the beach to create their own labyrinths fashioned from the natural materials close at hand and to enjoy the ceremony with her.

Walking the labyrinth is believed to increase right brain activity, and studies have shown that it actually balances the brain. I have found that even the most skeptical of those with whom I have shared the labyrinth find themselves feeling peaceful after the mindful walk.

Ceremony 3.5: Walking the Labyrinth

It is best to enter the labyrinth (as in any ceremony) with an intention.

> *Enter through the mouth or opening at the front of the labyrinth. Then walk on the paths or through the circuits. The walls, hedges, or markings keep you on course. It is said that when we reach the center we find God.*
>
> *It is a good idea to pause for a few minutes when arriving at the center to listen for messages. I love calling upon the Lady of the Labyrinth before entering. When reaching the center, I often quite clearly hear answers and messages in a feminine voice—the voice of the Lady.*

People often tell me that, shortly after a mindful walk in the labyrinth, they are able to make decisions and respond to changes with more acceptance and with more confidence than they could before their walk. When we participate in a ceremony such as walking the labyrinth with intention and by asking for help in finding answers, they virtually always come.

Sometimes angels of compassion, love, or peace appear. They may come in the form of a friend or helpful stranger whom we realize is offering the guidance and support we need. Or perhaps an e-mail shows up with information we are looking for. We only need to be open to receiving the answers. And movement ceremony—of any kind—facilitates that crucial openness.

From the moment of conception, a miraculous journey begins for a human body. As soon as we take our very first breath, new life—full of incredible new possibilities—embarks upon its unique course. Each of us has the innate capability to evolve in spirit, experience love and bliss, and make the absolute most of many opportunities.

Consider how our clay home develops. As the body forms inside a mother's uterus the spine is relatively straight. After birth, all of us kick and start to move around, creating more muscle tone and spinal flexibility. We then begin to crawl and our spine begins to develop a natural curve. The consequential correct alignment of the spine determines many things about our health throughout our lifetimes. As we learn to walk upright, for example, the spine continues to take shape in a manner that supports our amazing bodies and allows to move and function in the most efficient way possible. The spine is the key component of the skeleton, which is our physical foundation. Supported by the skeleton and covered and protected by our incredibly adaptable flesh, our spectacular organs allow us to breathe, eat, digest, eliminate, sense, think, and feel.

Whether we observe the wonderful human body and all it can do from the perspective of a medical student or an artist or simply someone who is curious, the complexity and perfection cannot be denied. The same Force that aligns the stars and planets also sweetly organizes everything in our clay homes—from the shape of our spine to the functioning of our lungs. We often take our bodies for granted—especially when our health is good. It is the responsibility of each of us, however, to take good care of our bodies/our clay homes, and a key component of that essential good care is frequent healthy movement.

Your body naturally longs for movement. If you notice children at play, they laugh freely, stretch often, and move around in an uninhibited state. Whether they are running, rolling in the grass, or climbing, it is the nature of healthy children to be in movement—not to simply sit still all day. They intentionally leave this natural state of movement only if they become sick. Follow the example of children. When you commit yourself to exercise and make frequent healthy movement a part of your life, you will be amazed by the benefits

I urge you to incorporate movement into your daily life and into the ceremonies that you may choose. Whether your movement comes in the form of a mindful walk early in the morning, a twenty-minute workout session at the local gym, or a solstice dance, integrate joyous movement into each day of your life.

It has been said that the 13th century Sufi poet, Rumi, created ecstatic dance—freeform movement expressing ecstasy. His words seem to serve as a most appropriate way to conclude this chapter about honoring our bodies through movement: "Dance, when you are broken open. Dance if you've torn the bandage off. Dance in the middle of the fighting. Dance when you are perfectly free."

Chapter 4

Releasing

"We must be willing to get rid of the life we've planned, so as to have the life that is waiting for us." ~ Joseph Campbell

We all bump into roadblocks in life from time to time. Addictions to coffee or junk food, mental obstacles created by low self-esteem, and self-imposed beliefs that stem from our childhood among other issues can get in the way of growth and happiness. If left unabated, life's roadblocks can become virtually impenetrable brick walls that can lead to divorce, health problems, depression, and other serious well-being issues

We all have the option, however, of clearing blockages, cleansing our bodies, and releasing negative energy along the way. When you create space in your life to participate in ceremony—whether it is the ritual of meditation or yoga or a special effort focused on letting go—you are anchoring yourself in Spirit. This anchoring allows you to stand strong through life's changes and challenges.

When releasing becomes part of a regular practice, many roadblocks can be managed and potential brick walls can be avoided. I am reminded of my childhood, when smoking was glamorized on television.

I became convinced that I should start smoking ... and so I did - - at age fifteen This was the first serious roadblock to well being that I created for mySelf and that, one day, would need to be confronted ... and released.

By the time I was seventeen, drug dependency had also become part of my personality. My loving mother had unfortunately become dependent on prescription drugs and shared them with me to help me "relax" in my early teens. By the time I was nineteen, I was convinced that I could not function without being in a chemically altered state to relieve my depression.

My mother had no idea what she was doing when she shared her medication with me, just as many contemporary parents do not realize the negative impact of allowing their children to spend most of their time playing video games or watching television. Consider what children and teens miss when they do not learn how to calm themselves down naturally, allowing themselves to develop into wonderful young men and women without the help of chemicals.

Moreover, drugs are frequently prescribed to children with learning disabilities or emotional turmoil, when a change in diet combined with more outdoor activity is often what they need. Listening to children with our hearts and allowing them to express the feelings they are experiencing gives them permission to be true to themselves. This simple act of listening can help them learn to work through their difficulties. Drugs only sidetrack them—and us—from connecting with Spirit and experiencing true happiness.

I left home at the ripe old age of seventeen, furious at my parents who had divorced and already dependent on drugs and tobacco. I was convinced that I was much smarter than my parents. I thought that leaving would hide all the hurt and heartbreak. Sooner or later, however, all of the negativity had to come out. At that time, I did not realize the gifts that were contained in overcoming difficulty—naturally. Without a desire to find personal freedom and some help from the angels, I would not have been as lucky as I was to develop the inner strength to break free.

Fortunately, I landed a pretty good job in a nice clothing store in Boston when I left home. At first, the manager told me he could not hire me because I was under eighteen. After I told him that I had moved to the big city on my own and sharing my experience of working since the age of fourteen, he finally agreed to give me a shot.

At the store, I met a wonderful friend who later told me that I was hired as her replacement. There is no doubt that a love from many lifetimes before had brought us together again in our youth and absence of wisdom. We were roommates for a couple of years until she met a man and moved to the South. I lived on my own for several months, until she contacted me and realized I was having problems.

I was not in a healthy state due to drugs. I had also gained fifty pounds and was miserable with the person I had become. With the encouragement of my friend, regular exercise, and a vegetarian diet of brown rice, lots of vegetables and fruits, and no junk food, I stopped using drugs and smoking. My friend also introduced me to yoga and meditation. I woke up every morning to quietly meditate and practice yoga. Her cat came to my door every morning like clockwork to sit with me during meditation. He would literally knock with his paw on my door to let me know he wanted to join me. (Animals know a good thing when it's happening!)

I had briefly become interested in meditation when reading some books about Zen Buddhism before I left home. Now I was ready to meditate. I began to touch on my own inner peace and find such joy upon entering that sanctuary daily.

I still find it incredible that meditation for only twenty minutes each day can truly change a person's life if they desire to be different or simply more at peace. Within six months, I lost fifty pounds. I found that by focusing on positive changes in my life and mySelf, I was able to let go of my destructive habits. I began to understand more about mySelf and I began to thrive. I began to love my life and to explore new possibilities.

Life constantly changes. Change is the nature of our being. Our cells, for example, are constantly renewing themselves. Nature—during her never-ending dance—reminds us about this phenomenon with the changing of the leaves or the continuous flow of the river. Let's consider the river: It is affected by many things such as temperature, animals, fish, people, boats, and the seasons. Yet the river is always pulling water from its sources to continue its flow. And within the flow of life, bliss and love are always available. Our guides and angels are always present to help us access this love and bliss. We only need to remember to ask. Love is our connection to Source.

It is the ego that resists change. It urges us to delude ourselves into feeling comfortable with old habits, toxic relationships, jobs that create stress, and unhealthy environments. Nevertheless, there is always a need to purify, cleanse, and shift to accept our true callings, to create more joy and peace in our lives, and, ultimately, in the world. If we change our habits—even in a small way—we begin to change our lives.

Stop to consider what you need to release in order to improve your energy levels, to purify your body, and to create new space to allow yourself new opportunities. This process may be uncomfortable at times, but, I assure you, the results will help you to embrace positive, new directions. You will find energy and confidence in your ability to adapt and shift into a healthier, happier life.

So, the question becomes: How do you change and clear? Remember: The small shifts make a difference. Taking a yoga class, for example, will begin to rejuvenate your body. As your energy increases, eating junk food and red meat, becomes less appealing. You begin to nourish your body with brightly colored fruits and vegetables, which make you feel even better. Feeling better, you will wake up earlier and more refreshed. Additionally, you will find that twenty minutes of morning meditation is easy to accomplish and makes you feel better all day.

For some people, these minor shifts may not seem to be so small. Nonetheless, in making these shifts and taking these steps, your life begins the all-important process of organic change.

Before long, you will begin to find yourself feeling as agile as a full-grown jaguar in a rare and beautiful rain forest ... ready to take a giant leap. One cannot take a huge leap of faith without first taking the required initial small steps. This is where ceremony comes in—and it must come from the heart. A ceremony such as a wedding or bar mitzvah, when attended by merely going through the motions, is simply ineffective. To make a real, lasting difference let your own heart and your intention guide you to make positive changes in your life, and let intention guide you to release that which is no longer healthy for you. Consider the following simple ceremonies to assist you in transforming your life and find what works for you.

Ceremony 4.1: Fire Ceremony (Letting Go with Fire)

Build a fire outside or in your fireplace. I often use something as simple as a candle inside a bowl or dish in my room or on a porch.

Choose what you want to release and find something to represent what you are letting go of. You may write it on paper or you may simply burn a twig or some leaves symbolic of what you are releasing—whether it is mental, emotional, or physical.

Spend some quiet time before you burn the item. Before you let it go, state how it (i.e., a job, relationship, addiction, difficulty) has served or taught you. It is important to honor yourself in this ceremony by burning something that represents a difficulty that you have learned from.

Perhaps the difficulty ultimately made you stronger; perhaps it made you realize that you are powerful; perhaps it made you fully realize that you deserve love.

Now burn the paper or object representing your release. Watch it burn. You may do this alone or with a loving witness. If you do not have a witness present, find someone you trust with whom to share the release after the ceremony.

During the next couple of days, find a way to celebrate your release.

You no longer need that which has been released in your life! You can sing a song, have lunch with a friend, or do a little dance in your room. In any case, be sure to make it an affirming recognition that a positive change has taken place in your life.

Intention and Release

Be clear about your intention. Are you releasing a relationship or simply the negative aspects of the relationship? Are you letting go of your job or finding a way to let go of old methods and behavior in regard to that job? I have witnessed situations in which letting go of fear and anxiety was all that individuals needed to move forward in their workplaces.

Above all, make sure you recognize and gain clarity about what you are letting go of before starting a releasing ceremony and take a few minutes to meditate on your intentions. Once you are clear about the element you wish to release and your intentions toward it, honor the teachings it brought you and be prepared to let it go. After each ceremony, be patient with yourself and focus on being free from past hindrances.

Again, remember: It is your intention that opens the path for ceremony to be effective. I suggest the following ceremony as a means of releasing. I have both participated in and witnessed this ceremony many times and find it to be very effective.

Ceremony 4.2: Seven Candles

Place seven white candles on silver candle holders. You can also use votive candles and place them on a coin such as an older silver dollar or an older quarter, which actually contain silver. (Silver is important here because it is said to neutralize negative energy).

The candles should be placed in a circle on the floor, in an open space that you can walk around freely. In the center of the circle place something that symbolizes what you are releasing. It could be a photo, an object, or simply a piece of paper on which you have written what you are letting go. Place the item in the center of the circle. You may also use a saucer of salt in the center if silver is not available. Salt is an excellent neutralizer of negative energy.

Now walk backwards or counter clockwise around the

circle of candles seven times. Each time you get back to the beginning point, say with authority, or yell if you like, one or all of these statements:

"I break you free from my consciousness."
"I am free and so are you."
"I no longer need this pattern in my consciousness."
"I set you free."

After any ceremony, there is a process of integration before you might feel totally free of the blockage. You may have to repeat Seven Candles three days in a row to have complete release. Sometimes you will notice the release immediately or you may simply feel that your energy is lighter. Always, as in the previous ceremony, take a few moments to honor what you have learned from this situation or relationship before you let it go.

Bear in mind that releasing is a process. It is not likely that you built up a feeling of negativity over night, even if it seems that way. It might take a few weeks for a release to complete itself after ceremony. You may also need more than one ceremony to feel a complete release as it peels away underlying emotions you were not aware of. That is perfectly fine.

There is no limit to the number of releasing ceremonies you can do. Each one gets rid of emotional toxins, frees up energy, and clears the way for new opportunities.

Ceremony 4.3: Fire Ceremony

When going through intense transition in your life, consider a fire ceremony. You may have only one or you may have one each week for up to four weeks. I like using four weeks because twenty-eight days is often said to be the amount of time it takes to break a habit. You can have a fire ceremony with a candle or using a fire in a fire bowl or fireplace.

Begin by selecting something to represent the attitude, habit, or relationship that you wish release. What you choose can be almost anything. A natural item such as a twig or small stick will work perfectly. To add energy and power to the ceremony, while the object burns and you consider your release, carefully run your hands through the flames and draw the energy of the fire into three of your major chakra areas: the naval area, the heart area, and the crown chakra area. For each area run your hands through the flames and pull the fire energy toward you—into the area of focus. I cannot explain why, but this action has a powerful effect in releasing unwanted negative energies and in promoting acceptance of the new person you desire to become.

Ceremony 4.4: Healing Ceremony for the Body

This is an easy ceremony to do when you are by yourself, lying in bed.

First, consider that the Celts believe the body is our clay home and that the soul resides both within and outside the body. The body dwells within the sphere of the soul until the clay home dies and the soul moves away from the body. The following ceremony encourages you to focus on a specific part of your body, which needs to be cleansed or healed from pain or affliction.

Lie down in a comfortable position and close your eyes. Imagine a brilliant light flowing over you and breathe in the light. Let the afflicted part of your body know that you are sorry for neglecting it and taking it for granted. Tell it that you are sending a beautiful, healing light from the soul to heal it.

After you inhale the soul light, imagine, as you exhale, breathing out residue from burnt coal as if you are exhaling dust or exhaust smoke. Continue this breathing for approximately five minutes. Continue speaking kindly to your body, letting the affected area know that you are sorry for neglecting it. Honoring your body in this way will soothe you and help you to heal.

Ceremony 4.5: Releasing Poverty Consciousness

Take a few minutes to consider what early childhood judgments or religious beliefs or attitudes about money might be holding you back from prosperity.

Write the beliefs down on paper and read aloud what you have written. Express what you have learned from these beliefs. Then, strongly assert that you no longer need any of these views that inhibit you from knowing prosperity. Burn the paper listing your old belief in a fireplace or tear up the paper and ... jump for joy!

Recognition of Miscarriage or Abortion

Every pregnancy that comes into a woman's life teaches her something. No matter how long the pregnancy lasts, the beginning of the embryo and the spirit of a child come to you for a reason.

As a medium, I have worked with many women who have miscarried or lost a child. It is my belief that we choose our parents and the exact time and place of our birth that is best for our souls' evolution. Obviously, this does not mean our lives will be without difficulty, but we do come into a life to learn the lessons that will help us evolve for the better.

And what can be said about abortion and the paralyzing sadness and guilt that so often accompany it? For reasons that we often do not totally understand, a choice is made to stop the pregnancy. If you have ever made this choice— for any reason—it is extremely important to set yourSelf free from the emotional and psychological prison that may have been created. You can accomplish this by releasing your guilt, sorrow, and/or anger for being unable to fulfill the role of mother or father to the unborn child.

Remember that the spirit of that child may come back to you at a later time or it may choose to be a part of a completely different family. In either case, the spirit continues to evolve for the better. No matter what your feelings may be toward the unborn child or yourSelf after terminating the pregnancy, it is essential that you take the time for sincere honoring and focused releasing through ceremony. Take the time to recognize the importance of your choice by honoring the unborn child.

If you have experienced a miscarriage, it is important to remember that miscarriage is never your fault. In my observation, a miscarriage is often the result of the spirit's deciding the time is not right for it to return to earth.

The following ceremony allows you to honor the presence of the spirit that was considering you as its parent and, consequently, to release any resentment or feelings of guilt that you may hold as a result of the loss.

Ceremony 4.6: Honoring the Unborn Child

Begin this ceremony by lighting a candle, playing soft music, or sitting outside in a beautiful place. Tell the spirit how the pregnancy made you feel by writing a letter or voicing your heartfelt thoughts. Take this time to speak from your heart to the spirit of the child that came into your life. You might want to name the spirit. Acknowledge the love you have for the spirit and ask for the highest good for that entity. You might feel sadness, anger, guilt, confusion, or a mixture of any/all of these emotions. There are no wrong feelings in this situation.

When you are ready to release your ties and let the spirit of the child move on, wish it happiness, and tell the child/spirit to find joy. The key is to let it all go – completely and absolutely.

I believe each spirit that comes to us—whether to grow up and become the child that will have our grandchildren or to be the child who we cannot keep—has purpose in our lives and on this Earth. We must be certain to honor each such experience with love.

The Mayans have a beautiful tradition of dedicating their children to Father Sky as the true Father and Mother Earth as the true Mother. In the ceremony, they recognize their own parenthood simply as being temporary guardians for their children. The true parents are Father Sky and Mother Earth. Each child comes to fulfill his or her own destiny and to take a path separate from ours.

I believe this is a much healthier way of accepting parenthood than the concept often embraced in Western cultures, and in North America in particular. Parents in these societies often cling to their children long past the time needed. This enables them to become dependent and unable to seek their own paths or develop strength by making mistakes for which they must take personal responsibility

As parents and grandparents, we must totally embrace our precious responsibility of guiding and caring for our children. It is important that we give them spiritual roots and direction to become responsible adults with values and integrity. And we must also to step back and allow these beings to find their own paths. They came into this world with a purpose, just as we did. We must let go of the lofty plans we may have fantasized for them and listen with the heart to their desires. Our task is to act as our children's and grandchildren's guardians— with love and respect.

Personal releasing ceremonies are wonderful when shared with friends or witnesses, but they can also be very effective when performed when you are by yourself. Never underestimate the power of these simple ceremonies. As you release old habits or patterns, new energy is available which attracts wonderful new opportunities for personal growth, health, and fulfillment of your greatest dreams.

Within each ceremony for release, we surrender our old ways and allow ourselves to become new. Through the discipline of going into a sacred space each day through the ritual of prayer, meditation, or personal ceremony, you can become enlivened and more aware of what your body needs as well as the opportunities for change and increased awareness that are available.

Small shifts in thinking and in releasing negative feelings will ultimately help you to make quantum leaps. When the quantum leap does occur, you will realize that you have been propelled through a door into a new life, which holds many surprises. Suddenly, you will find yourself standing with the partner of your dreams or being ready to begin a new business. Or you may strongly sense your readiness to start a new career that you have always imagined as fulfilling your passions. Or you may be poised to embark upon any other dream—one that you cannot even imagine at this moment. All you have to do is have the courage to accept that your dreams can come true and allow yourSelf to take the leap.

It is my hope that you realize that, if you align yourSelf with all that is true to the being that you are, only good will come. Ceremony can help you change your life. It is as ancient as time. Our ancestors honored the sunrise, built fires to celebrate an abundant harvest, and danced to honor the passing of a loved one's life. Your very cells contain memories of great ceremonies in which you and your ancestors have previously participated.

In beginning to embrace the ceremonies of release discussed in this chapter, step gingerly as a child learning to walk, and let each day fill you with wonder. As you take baby steps through your initial meditation and simple practice of the ceremonies and rituals that resonate with you, you learn to walk and even dance. In reaching this state, your awareness will always lead you to the fulfillment of your heart's desire.

Chapter 5

Forgiveness. Finding the Peace Within.

"The weak can never forgive. Forgiveness is an attribute of the strong."
~ Mahatma Gandhi

We all encounter situations when forgiving feels difficult and sometimes impossible, but harboring resentment, anger, or hatred blocks us from receiving Good in our lives.

You may not want to continue a relationship with someone who has caused you pain. In ending that relationship, however, letting go of the remnants of the anger and bitterness, guilt or shame that remain is important to both your peace of mind and your health. Those emotions, if not addressed, become negative entities. Looking at forgiveness in a holistic sense gives your body, mind, and spirit a fresh start.

Consider the energetic impact, which takes place within your luminous spirit body—the light that connects us to all living things—when you forgive absolutely, and in so doing release negative entities. Each entity develops its own life. And, having life, each entity has a form of will—the will to remain alive and embodied in its host. Consequently, it takes real effort to cast out negative entities.

Moreover, if you feel that it can be a hugely daunting challenge to forgive at times, it is very likely that you are actually experiencing the strength of a negative entity, whose continued existence can block you from receiving your Good and being able to forgive. We sometimes call this force a demon or a negative emotional entity. Unless we take immediate measures to neutralize such entities or to free ourselves from them, they can eventually cause illness in the physical body. More important than anything, you must love yourSelf enough to forgive who you have become as a result of harboring negative entities.

Years ago, my family underwent a heart-wrenching experience, the details of which I cannot release here in order to protect the innocent. I was filled with anger and bitterness at the thought of what had happened to the person I love. Hatred grew and filled my heart with misery. I constantly projected thoughts that reflected this anger and bitterness. At times, I even fantasized about the death of the person who was responsible for the pain. I was never at peace.

My anger spawned more anger and much bitterness. I fed it and suffered great anxiety created by my inability to deal with my pain and emotions in a better way. Finally, I decided to go on a vision quest and deal with the anger and resentment within mySelf.

A few days before that quest, I dreamed with amazing clarity. I dreamed of a crystal clear mountain stream sparkling in the sun. Attempting to hide within the stream, however, was a deadly poisonous snake. Upon awakening, I immediately realized that the stream was within my own heart and soul and the snake was the anger and bitterness, which was poisoning me. Later, on the quest, I freed myself of the poisonous snake hiding within my heart. I cried many tears and listened to the words and wisdom of a spiritual guide who helped free me from the anger and bitterness. I willed myself to be open to clearing the negative emotions because I could not find peace any other way.

Sometimes life brings us situations or events that are totally out of our control. We may lose loved ones to accident or sickness or have great storms of change that cause us heartache and difficulties. With each situation, we must find a way to cry our tears, yell out, or express feelings of anger and frustration. And then, we must find a way to let go of those feelings that block us from experiencing joy. Having truly forgiven, we will be able to open up to life's miracles of change.

We are the only ones who can free our own Selves. And to do this we must first recognize the presence of the negative emotion. Only then will we have the power to free ourSelves with help from angels of peace and love. Often we are helpless to control what bad things may happen to us, or those whom we love, but we must forgive those responsible in order to regain our sense of peace and balance. It makes sense to do a ceremony specifically for this purpose. Whether your ceremony takes fifteen minutes or you devote a quest to the cause, it will greatly benefit you and those close to you.

Forgiving Hurtful Relationships

It is important that we take a close look at the nature of the people with whom we spend our time. Some people cannot be trusted. Those who in their very nature are not trustworthy are bound to disappoint us. Being aware of the potential lack of integrity in some people does not mean we should condemn them. Nor does it ever condone abusive or destructive behavior. We should be ready, however, to surrender to an awareness that those who consistently disappoint us are incapable of loving consistently. We must replace the negative energy we feel toward such people with love, harmony, and peace. Through doing this, we let go of the toxic emotions festering in our own energetic bodies.

A friend of mine came to me years ago because her husband of two decades had betrayed her. It was not the first time that he had found another, she admitted; it had happened twice before. She was heartbroken and asked my advice.

"Kick him out, of course," I said. (She made him leave shortly thereafter).

After receiving some counseling in her hometown, however, my friend decided that her husband could move back in. Sadly, he left her several years later for a woman young enough to be my friend's daughter. One could furiously shake a condemning finger at him, but the truth is that he had made it very clear early on that he could not be trusted. You cannot leave a hawk in a rabbits' pen and expect them to be friends: Ultimately, you can only expect to find no rabbits.

We are all responsible for our own thoughts, how we handle our emotions, and, ultimately, how we make our own choices. It is important to recognize our responsibility for own feelings when we are angry at a spouse or friend for thoughtlessness or betrayal. Perhaps they simply had to find a way out of the relationship or were incapable of the responsibilities inherent in having a close friendship.

We must take on the responsibility to forgive and let go in order to live in a state of gratitude and abundance. Only the individual person has the ability to be responsible for allowing himself or herself happiness. No other person or situation can bring happiness. And this means that we must love ourSelves enough to honor and be true to who we are.

The only things in life we have any real control over are our own thoughts and choices. Our thoughts create our lives on a daily basis. When we feel good and focus on blissful thoughts and feelings, life brings us fulfillment. When we do not, life becomes unbalanced.

Practicing Forgiveness

Catholics have a time for practicing forgiveness; they call it absolution. You do not have to be part of the Catholic faith, however, to obtain absolution. Through the expression of forgiveness to a loving recipient, you show a willingness and ability to forgive not only yourSelf but also someone else who may not even be aware that you are forgiving him or her. It is important, however, to trust the person that you admit your feelings to. In the case of doing any ceremony for yourSelf, it is best to have someone you trust to share it with—even if the sharing comes after the fact.

After years of my experiencing a distant relationship with my mother, she had a stroke. The woman who had brought me into the world was suddenly at the edge of death. Our relationship had been almost nonexistent for years. I had previously rationalized that I could not possibly feel close to someone who, or so many years, had chosen drugs before me and her family.

When I decided to visit her, my heart was broken to see this lady—hardly capable of speech—work so hard to tell me that she loved me. Then, my heart became open and welcoming as she returned to an emotionally present woman who was ready and willing to share her feelings with her only daughter. Through months of my mother's physical recovery and roller coaster ride between improvement and decline, our relationship healed. Through love, anything can heal—if only we allow it.

One day while she was recovering, my mother told me how sorry she was for the hurt she had caused me. I had already forgiven her but still needed to accept the forgiveness that she asked for and the love she offered me. I told her that because of the difficulties I had experienced in our family, I had become a better counselor and had developed more compassion for others. She knew that she was forgiven. Magic words then came to me from my mother: "We love each other." This simple declaration was music to my ears.

In life, we have choices to make each day. We can choose to feel good and connect to our real feelings or we can choose to be victims and become bitter and unhappy. Everyone has wounds from life's events and from some of the people whom we love. It is whether or not we choose to heal from these wounds that matters. We must find the bittersweet piece of the puzzle that makes us whole and brings us back to our hearts.

Whether you need a vision quest to forgive some deeply difficult situation or a very simple ceremony, you will find that, through a ceremony of forgiveness, great joy awaits you and that there are many unimaginable ad very pleasant surprises in store along the way.

Finding Peace Through Ceremony

Forgiveness may come instantly, almost easily, or it may take a great deal of effort, requiring more than one ceremony. Remember, when intentionally forgiving, through the practice of ceremony, you are grounding the abstract masculine into the feminine earth, which can take time.

The negative emotional entities must be banished. They can linger and remain close at times, waiting for a moment to jump back in. Be gently but constantly aware of yourSelf as you remain alert for the signs that another ceremony is needed. It is important to recognize that sometimes you need more than one ceremony to respond to a specific issue.

Ultimately, forgiving will cleanse your spirit and open you up to receiving the good you deserve. Forgiveness, however, can be extremely difficult to give and the forgiving process may stir up many emotions. Make sure you practice a ceremony for forgiveness until you have released any and all negative feelings and know that you are ready to let go—completely, absolutely. It is also important to identify specifically what and who you are forgiving and go into the ceremony committed to the intention to forgive.

Try any of the following ceremonies to forgive yourSelf or someone else. The entire process usually takes more than a little time—from several days to about several weeks—to fully integrate the experience. For serious difficulties, start with the letter technique (Ceremony 5.1) and follow up with a fire ceremony for four weeks, doing one ceremony each week.

It stands to reason that having deep-rooted negative feelings sometimes takes even more work, more digging to let go and forgive than with less intense feelings. Pay attention to life's cues and you will be guided.

Ceremony 5.1: Letter of Forgiveness

Sit down with a pen and paper or your computer and keyboard. Pour out, in writing, any sadness or pain in your heart. Tell the person you want to forgive how he/she hurt you. Write what you have learned about yourself as a result of this difficult experience. Here is a simple outline to get you started:

> *This is what you did;*
> *This is how it made me feel;*
> *This is how your actions have affected my life.*

When you are finished, read the letter aloud to yourself or to witnesses. Then—and this is extremely important—wish peace upon the person who caused you pain ... and burn the letter. (You can build a fire in something as simple as a cake pan if you do not have access to an outdoor flame.) You can also release the letter in a body of water. (In this case, write your letter on environmentally friendly rice paper before sending it off). Breathe deeply as you watch the letter burn or dissolve.

Ceremony 5.2: Three Letter Ceremony

When you are ready to forgive, write three letters in a day or within several days.

Begin by writing a letter to the person you want to forgive. Tell how he/she hurt you and let any anger, sadness, disappointment, betrayal, or pain flow onto the page.

Next, write a letter from the perspective of the person you are forgiving. Think about how the relationship made him/her feel and why he/she reacted in certain ways that hurt you.

Then, write a third letter from an objective point of view- - as if you were a newspaper reporter focusing on the facts of the situation.

When you are finished, read the letters aloud to yourself or to witnesses. Find the strength to wish peace to the person whom you are forgiving.

Now, you will need to build a fire. You may build it in something as simple as a cake pan if you don't have access to an outdoor flame. Burn the letters. Or, once again being mindful of the environment, you can also release the letters in water if an ocean or lake, for example, is nearby.

Breathe deeply as you watch the letters burn or dissolve.

When you have completed the previous steps, it is time to celebrate. This last step is a very important part of the ceremony. Celebrate by playing a song, dancing, taking a friend to lunch, toasting your new peace, or any other way that seems fitting for you. This final act of celebration will help give you closure.

Ceremony 5.3: Forgiving with Tears

A young client had great success with the following ceremony. She was in a strained relationship, which left her continually feeling upset and insecure. She finally recognized that she needed to release something about herself in order to find forgiveness. I asked her to enumerate the fears, sadness, disappointment, and regrets that were causing her so much sadness and to cry into a bowl of water and she did so.

Two months after participating in this ceremony and releasing her anguish, my client became engaged to the man she loved and, in doing so, found great peace in her relationship with him.

Use a bowl that means something to you, perhaps a ceramic bowl or piece of pottery. Add some fresh water to the bowl and set it next to you. Then light a candle and place it beside the bowl.

Begin the ceremony by expressing silently or aloud any grief or regrets. Tell the water your sadness and let your tears fall into the water. When you feel that all the tears have fallen, reflect upon what you have learned from the experience. Forgive yourself and get ready to move on. Then, pour the water out and wash your hands.

Honoring the Journey

We enter into the world—the sweet journey we call life—with our very hearts and souls connected to the creation of all living things. We are all children of Creator and only lose touch with that bliss and beauty as pain and wounding/injury cause us to block out and sometimes disconnect from Spirit.

Through this sacred journey, we each have the opportunity to reconnect. We need to be mindful that Creator longs to embrace us as much as we longed for the sweet embrace of our mother's arms when we were children.

Accept every opportunity to know your own sweet soul, for yours is part of a vast and wondrous Creation. Remember that no other individual is like you. If you are not happy with who you are now, allow yourself to change. Age or money or education make no difference. When you look back over your life and consider no longer being here, think about your legacy. Consider the notion of leaving behind no anger, bitterness, or resentment; leave only as much love and laughter as you can muster.

I encourage you to consider your life as a song. As you observe the sparrow or mockingbird singing, you can see the chest swelled in a true expression of joy. Within each of us there is a beautiful song, longing to be expressed. That song is an integral component of the sacred journey that is our life—a life that passes so quickly before we move on to another world.

How will you honor your journey? Are you willing to take the risk of loving like you never have before? Are you willing to listen to all the voices within you and to honor each in a way that lets you be true to yourSelf? Are you ready to forgive—others and yourSelf?

You may come to answers to these questions through one or more of the ceremonies offered so far, or you may consider embarking upon a vision quest.

Chapter 6

Vision Quest.
Embracing Rites of Passage.

"The clearest way into the Universe is through a forest wilderness."
~ John Muir

Throughout history, ceremonial rites of passage have helped people through life transitions. The bible tells us of Jesus fasting in the wilderness for forty days to confront His demons, seek wisdom from God, and prepare Himself for a bold new phase in life. Even in our contemporary world, ceremonial rites of passage are still practiced. Many indigenous tribes have special ceremonies to initiate young men or women into adulthood, for example. Right of passage such as these exist because the cultures that host them believe profoundly that transitional times must be honored.

Rites of passage represent an initiation into the next phase of life. One of my Native American friends tells me that the vision quest is intended to clear the way for the new to come to us. Embarking upon a vision quest can help remind us that we come into this world with special gifts and an inner design to guide us to the path of spirit. In our very first breath is a commitment to this life, which comes from purity and bliss. We are part of an infinite cosmos, connected to Creator, and born in total innocence. All that we experience from our birth from this life and past lives—good and bad, pain and joy—makes us the truly unique human beings that we are.

Ahead of all of us are opportunities to shift in our thoughts and in our actions. These simple changes to find our truths, this desire to connect to Spirit as much as possible, can and will change our lives.

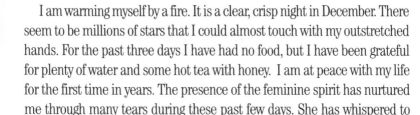

I am warming myself by a fire. It is a clear, crisp night in December. There seem to be millions of stars that I could almost touch with my outstretched hands. For the past three days I have had no food, but I have been grateful for plenty of water and some hot tea with honey. I am at peace with my life for the first time in years. The presence of the feminine spirit has nurtured me through many tears during these past few days. She has whispered to me special words about the love and safety she promises that I will find in my work. Last night when I came back to my tent, my heart skipped as I saw a beautiful gigantic angel standing beside my fire. I fell to my knees and cried because it was the first time that I had actually seen her. She told me that she had always been with me, and, in my heart, I knew this to be true.

The preceding paragraph is a rendering of the first vision quest/wilderness fast that I experienced. It came within a year of my divorce. I was miserable and searching for a way to heal my heart and the emotional pain that I had experienced. A divorce is, itself, certainly a rite of passage, which can take us on a journey from one period of our lives into another. Mine certainly did. My vision quest was my opportunity to balance the rite of passage that I experienced during my divorce with what I was hoping to transition to as a new, independent, strong, and highly energized single woman. At that time, I made it my mission to grow from my divorce and face midlife with all of its challenges.

On the Sunday before my quest, I enjoyed a day of canoeing with some friends. As I pulled the canoe onto the riverbank, something glittered in the water. I reached out to pick up a rock. I showed it to my friend who said "Oh my gosh, it's a heart!" I realized that the hand-sized rock was shaped exactly like a heart. My guide and mentor for the vision quest had suggested, a few days earlier, that in preparation for our upcoming trip we find an object symbolizing what the vision quest would be for us. Without a doubt, this rock was my symbol for that quest for it was on that quest that I found my own true heart.

———◆◆———

Now in some Native American tribes individuals sit in a circle on their chosen site while an elder keeps watch over the area. Each member on the quest draws a circle around his or her space and does not leave this Sacred Circle for the time period designated. In these cultures, it is said that no participant in the vision quest may look upon the face of any other person who is questing. This is a time for complete focus on one's personal relationship with Creator.

Some tribes quest with no food or water although the quests I have been on always require water. While I respect that there are many different methods for questing, I know that one does not have to go without water to have visions. And refraining from hydration can, of course, create serious health concerns.

I have experienced and witnessed more healing from quests than my words can express. For each person who participates, this rite of passage allows a true and deep transformation to take place. It is during this time that one cries tears that beg to be shed and one feels pain and anguish that have never been acknowledged. And, perhaps most important, it is a time for one to confront the fear of the ego's surrender as it gives way to spirit and higher cause.

When that ego surrenders, it may feel like death and may be terrifying, but it is only a temporary surrender. After a quest, the ego snaps back with amazing resilience, but the surrender creates a new awareness of the difference between ego desires and heart and soul desires. When you listen to your heart very carefully during a quest, you will discover answers to extremely important questions and you will experience much joy.

Imagine the freedom of being alone with yourself—free to feel and experience anything. As a mentor of mine always said, "Remember the ancient Samurai warriors mantra: 'Expect nothing, be ready for anything'." I have found that this advice is constantly applicable during every vision quest I have been associated with.

It can take months to prepare for a vision quest. Preparation involves mindfully committing to a period of fasting and deep inner work as you enter a state dedicated to the intention of denying the ego. During a vision quest, the ego will often kick and fight as it tells us that we have to eat. It brings up fears of darkness and even monsters. As you settle into your quest, however, you begin to realize the monster is actually your own ego. So you seek a way to tame the beast. And, while it should be tamed, it should not be forever destroyed. After all, we need our ego. It is a practical necessity. It reminds us to pay our bills, it helps us to keep a good income coming in, and it pushes us to accomplish many other necessary things.

Through a vision quest, we learn balance—to give our ego less importance. The peace that comes with that surrender is amazing. Through it, we can learn to recognize the difference between the voice of the ego and the calling of the soul. While the ego can help us acquire a beautiful living space, motivate us to keep track of our finances, and assist us in looking attractive; the soul can bring us to our true path in life. The calling from our soul fulfills us in a way we cannot fully realize until we respond to that calling, which can occur only if we allow the ego to stand aside.

One rite of passage that contemporary American culture unfortunately often fails to recognize is entry into adulthood. Most American children rarely receive guidance from elders on how to become adults—even though, around the ages of eighteen to twenty-one, they reach a phase when they are certainly ready to give up childhood, to let the ways of childhood die. The problem is that they often do not know how to do this.

During late adolescence, the soul yearns for initiation and acceptance into adulthood. It wants to shed its old self and blossom into a young man or woman. Many young people do not understand how to channel their building desires to make such a radical change. And often, they do not receive guidance from a parent or mentor to help them acknowledge and honor their souls' desires. The void of a ceremonial rite of passage to initiate children into adulthood is one of the biggest reasons so many young people in our society turn to destructive initiation activities: gangs, drug use, or, far worse, suicide.

Most indigenous tribes have rites of passage of childhood into adulthood. Many ceremonies are elaborate and some dangerous. These ceremonies create an opportunity for the individual to experience an ego death so that the young person can surrender into a new life as an adult with more responsibility. A vision quest is often used for this particular rite of passage.

As I suggested previously, mainstream American society has, to a large extent, moved away from ceremony. Consequently, life itself—aside from an individual's willing and deliberate participation in an appropriate ceremony—often creates devastating, unplanned rites of passage through illness, divorce, and sometimes death. Nevertheless, many other cultures are still rich with the practice of ceremony with all of its very important practical effects. For example, seeking a method of practicing ceremony to represent the temporary death of the ego is, of course, always preferable to an actual physical death.

On one of my vision quests, I surrendered my old fears and mental blocks of remembering experiences from previous lives in another world. During this experience of Self-actualization, a part of my soul returned—only to fill me with all the love and joy that I had left behind with the other-worldly part of me. There were voices from guides and angels helping me to understand why I was on this journey, and I was reminded of my spirit name, which is Moruda.

When I heard this name in a vision, it resonated with my other-world memories and in my heart. I was very aware of Moruda's return into my being and I cried many tears at how I had pushed back that part of me because of my own frightened ego. Since integrating her into my consciousness, I have regained the ability to unconditionally love and accept who I am.

As I mentioned earlier, I have met with so many others who have memories and visions of different worlds. These other-world memories are really no different from memories of incredible events and life-changing situations in this lifetime that many others are eager to acknowledge. While some of us do have memories of other worlds, we must recognize and learn to accept and nurture our lives on Earth—as humans—here with a purpose. Let this understanding help you to be kind and loving and to keep your journey sacred. The world—the here and now—in which we live is rich and always offering wonderfully fresh experiences and brave new opportunities for growth.

While a vision quest is a traditional way of seeking initiation, you may choose some other type of trip or expedition as a rite of passage. Do so consciously and go with the intention of shedding the ego, or, as I like to say, dying to an old way of life. Give yourself the time and space to consider: Who am I? What am I becoming? What is my spirit name?

A while back, a friend of mine felt called to travel to New Zealand, Australia, and Southeast Asia for almost a year. During his journey, great healing took place for him. He unexpectedly found many new friends. While traveling, he discovered a new and different part of himSelf while letting go of other past issues that he discovered were inhibiting him. He paid attention to the call of his soul and let his intuition guide him in a new way.

———————●●———————

While he was away, a new opportunity for Self discovery revealed itself to him. In many ways, his journey led him to make a quantum leap. While he did not go into the wilderness to camp, many of the elements of a vision quest were fundamental components of his experience: courage, risk, intention, willingness to change, and being open to the unknown.

When you decide to embark on a quest—no matter where it might take you—please first consider all safety factors. If you are camping in the wilderness, go with someone who has wilderness experience. As an alternative, you may want to create a quest experience from the comfort and silence of a lodge.

A vision quest commonly lasts one to four days, but preparation for the quest may take months. Vision quests require us to push our egos aside for a short time just before or just after the ceremonies involved. You will want to spend time listening to the voices of your guides and ancestors as the quest's start date approaches. Some ceremonies may be performed before the quest and will encourage you to share sacred truths, bond with your intentions, and receive support as you prepare to embark on this special rite of passage. I have shared one of these (below) along with other actual vision quest ceremonies that I have used, and I urge you to pay attention to any callings to explore them further.

Ceremony 6.1: Severance Ceremony

This ceremony is used before the vision quest and is most effective when people in addition to those going on the quest attend. The purpose is to sever ties with the community as the seekers prepare to enter the wilderness.

> *The ceremony begins by forming a Sacred Circle (please refer to chapter 2) where community members present gifts that they would like to send with each person going on the quest. They may send prayers, blessings, protective herbs, or guidance for each individual. Each person going on the quest hears from each person in the circle. This lets the seekers know they are individually supported. It is not uncommon for the community members of the Sacred Circle to come to new understandings about themselves and/or share similar feelings with quest seekers as their journeys are about to begin.*

Ceremony 6.2: Vow of Silence

When you arrive at your wilderness designation, seek out a personal space that feels sacred to you. Some prefer to sit in the open or have a lean-to, while others bring a small tent. It is best to have no phones, reading material, or cameras to distract you from connecting to nature and pure intention. Remember: The weight of the pack you bring represents what you carry through life.

> *After setting up your sacred space, return to your initial meeting place and form a circle with your companions. Express your intention for going on the quest and voice the thoughts from your heart. Next, take a vow of silence with*

everyone on the quest. From this point on, no one speaks to anyone else until the quest has been completed.

Ceremony 6.3 Blessing Seven Directions

Go to your campsite and draw a circle in the earth around the entire area, with the exception of an open pathway where you can enter and exit the site without crossing the bounds of the circle. Place a shell or symbol in each of the four traditional directions.

> *Call North: where the cold is, where the frozen truth lies. Call East: where the sun rises, where new birth and creatures and humans are born. Call West: where the rains come from, where the thunderstorms build. Call South: where the heat comes from and the sun shines, where the fire heats up.*
>
> *Next ... Call Above: where our ancestors reside, where the sky people live. Call Below (to the animal kingdom): where all creatures great and small abide. Call Within: where the truth of the heart and soul resides. Call on the help of all the elements and all Creation. Call on archetypal energies used for thousands of years to protect and guide you. Then... sit and listen.*

You may notice that your skin feels more comfortable as you sit in silence in the open air. As you sit alone with your true Self, possibly for the first time since childhood, the ego will begin to surrender and release itself and allow the still spirit voice from within to be heard, to be felt. Space feels timeless.... It could be 2012 or 1400, and you will recognize silence as a friend to the soul.

In silence come tears, which need to be cried; laughter, which needs to

85

be heard; angels who desire to speak. The silence enables your heart to listen as answers begin to form and your true calling becomes more apparent. This is a time to come to terms with great pain and sorrow. It is a time to heal.

It is in this place that new energy and visions enter. The heart opens to an environment embraced by the arms of the great Mother Earth. Her hands of hills and valleys cradle the child who has returned to her womb.

Ceremony 6.4: Death Watch (Ceremony for Last Night of the Quest)

This ceremony is very powerful and should be entered into with only the most serious intent. The ceremony is to invite others metaphysically to visit you as if you were dying. What would others share with you if you were dying? Who would be there? Remember, the quest is about dying to an old way and surrendering to spirit through a temporary death of the ego.

Project the thought that you are inviting anyone who wishes to attend your Death Watch at a chosen time (for example, at sunset). Send this thought out throughout the day and afternoon. The silent invitation may be to those who are living or those who have passed; it may be sent to someone from your memories or visions; it may be sent to someone whom you may not yet know.

Build a small fire in your area. You can use a candle if you cannot build a fire. As you go to the area you have designated to await your visitors, send out the thought: The Door to my Death Watch is Open....

Now wait as long as you like and listen to the voices of family, friends, ancestors, and people who may surprise you with messages of love, regret, desire for forgiveness, and insight.

Thank each one who comes to you and feel free to express feelings or ask questions. You may wait up all night or for a couple hours. When you feel ready to stop, simply state: The Door of my Death Watch is Closed.

You will be amazed at the knowledge you gain and personal healing that takes place from this ceremony. Personally, I have experienced healing results soon after completing this ceremony. Others have shared with me that the Death Watch Ceremony was an incredible experience giving them great insights into themselves and many relationships.

Ceremony 6.5: Incorporation Ceremony

When you get back home from the quest, it is important to have a ceremony to rejoin the community. Often, the people from the community who shared in the severance ceremony have dreams or hunches about those on the quest.

Meet your community in a Sacred Circle and listen to their messages. You will likely find synchronicity between their thoughts and your experience. Then, deliver any gifts you have for them. You may have found a rock or feather or simply have a heartfelt thought that needs to be shared. The bond you will feel is a gift of spirit. It is a true new relationship between your heart and theirs that is rare and timeless.

You may emerge from the vision quest very different from your former personality. Learn to love who you are and what you have become. Inner peace is the result of listening and acting upon your own inner guidance.

Remember that the ego can be quick to attempt old habits. The gifts that come from a quest can take weeks, months, or even years to become completely integrated. However, the work must continue through meditation, prayer, and ceremony. We can always draw upon our deep inner source when we allow ourselves the time and silence to do so.

Should you decide to go on a quest, do so with reverence and good planning. Native Americans tell us that Earth is both our Mother and our Grandmother and that our spiritual practice will reach the next seven generations. We must honor and respect the Earth for she is a living being who has cared for us and provided for us in spite of our negligence and abuse of her. Without her, we would not have this life. My point is to be sure to incorporate thankfulness to Gaia as part of your ceremonies while seeking your quest.

We must create our own spiritual communities within the towns and cities where we reside. People who care for each other and speak from the heart are essential if we are to change our world. The vision quest is not for the faint of heart. We go with a deep understanding that we will never be the same again. We come back to our community with the gift of new life. There is an intimacy shared with fellow quest seekers that provides a lifetime link with sacred community.

Some nights stay up till dawn as the moon sometimes does for the sun. Be a full bucket, pulled up the dark way of a well then lifted into the light. Something opens our wings, something makes boredom and hurt disappear. Someone fills the cup in front of us, we taste only sacredness ~ Rumi

Chapter 7

Crossing Over

"When you realize how perfect everything is you will tilt your head back and laugh at the sky." ~ Hindu Prince Siddharta Gautama, the founder of Buddhism 563-483BC

It is approximately five thousand years ago in the land now known as Ireland. I am with a group of men and women from a small community. It is bitter cold. I can hear a small child crying as we approach the entrance of a tomb-like edifice. It took the engravers months of work to complete the marks in the stone. It has recently been completed.

We enter the chamber with a torch to light the way. A small animal scurries out. We walk to the inner chamber trying to warm ourselves. Close to my heart, I hold a small bundle. As we walk across the quartz floor, we gently place our stillborn baby on a crystal slab and huddle together to ward off the chill. We wait quietly in the dark, waiting for the sun to shine and free her spirit in this time of winter solstice. I ask myself: "How long will it take? Will the sun return as it has before?"

Silently we pray. Tears fall as sunlight gently slips through the cold stone passageway. The powerful light comes closer and gets stronger. Then, in a flash, the crystal walls and ceiling of the inner chamber are illuminated. The crystal clear quartz emits constant vibrations as it exudes incredible energy that feels very purifying. At that moment, we know the child is at peace and has left this Earth to continue her journey.

The events depicted above are a past life memory I recalled while visiting Ireland a few years ago. During our trip, I entered an historic landmark called New Grange that archaeologists date back five thousand years. It is well known for the winter solstice when a narrow beam of sunlight shines directly into a small slit in the thick stone of the chamber door for seventeen minutes each year. During this time, the quartz that makes up the chamber floor emits beautiful colors. Archaeologists suspect that the sunlight entering the passageway of the chamber, precisely on the winter solstice, was intended to help people buried in the tomb transition to the other side.

Inside the tomb, beads and pendants made of bone and beautifully polished stone have been found amidst human remains. In the center of the chamber sits a slab, or table, made of quartz. Archaeologists also believe it may have held the body of the deceased as their spirit was released from the earth during the solstice.

When I visited the chamber, I could not determine if bodies were laid alone on the crystal slab or if people were in the room with them. That is when my past life memory so clearly came to me. It must have been incredible, I now imagine—waiting inside the tomb, waiting for the sun to illuminate the inner chamber, waiting for confirmation that our loved one had peacefully passed on. After visiting the chamber in this lifetime and receiving such clarity, I left this incredible place feeling fully refreshed.

The amount of time and labor that went into constructing this amazing site gives us some insight into the significance their culture placed on burial rituals. Imagine the planning and labor that went into the construction of this incredible space for honoring and helping people transition to the other side.

Letting Go of Fear

We all fear the unknown, but the mystery of death and the afterlife is part of our life on this planet. We enter the light of the world from the secure darkness of our mother's womb. Birth is sacred as we take our first breath into an unknown world. Death is equally sacred as we leave the earth we have come to know and enter the doorway to eternity. We take our last precious breath to be embraced by the Great Mystery. As birth deserves celebration and announcement, so does our departure from our clay home—this body that has carried us through our world.

When it comes to death, no one really knows what happens, and every culture treats it differently. Ancient Egyptians created a symbolic door and placed scales in front of the body so the soul could weigh itself. They believed that the soul must be as light as a feather to go into the next world.

I once heard a psychologist speak to a group about grieving and ceremony. He told us that the tribe that he originated from in Africa celebrated for three days when someone died. The members of the tribe danced, played music, and cried. They believe that their tears formed a river to carry their loved one to the other side. He also mentioned that our contemporary American society discourages crying. He suggested that we must get back in touch with our hearts and allow the tears to flow for it is through crying our tears and feeling hidden pain that we are able to free ourSelves.

Whether you offer a simple prayer or participate in an elaborate celebration, the journey to the other side is sacred. Too often, I see people avoid any talk of death and pretend that everything is fine as close friend or family members draw closer to their last breath. Knowing that you are about to lose someone you love can be heartbreaking. Saying good-bye is never easy. But, you can honor and respect this transition by sending love and peace to the soul taking its journey, even though you will miss the departed in this life.

———————◆●◆———————

My grandfather was a wonderful man whose smiling blue eyes made me feel secure and loved. He knew hard work, having raised seven children on a farm and living off the land. He walked on crutches for most of his life after being run over by a tractor when he was young, but that did not stop him from having a full life.

My grandparents were married for more than fifty years. He had been in a lot of pain when he passed at the age of eighty-four. My aunt was sitting with him that night. As she nodded off, he teased her and woke her up. They began to laugh. Then, he looked up and said, "There's Christ." As soon as his words were spoken, he was gone. Knowing that he had left this world in the arms of Christ has brought me a peace and reassurance about death since I heard the story more than thirty years ago.

———————◆●◆———————

I cherish the stories told to me by people who were present when the spirit of their loved one turned to say good-bye after leaving the body. A family came to me several yeas ago after losing their daughter of forty-three years (we'll call her Sarah) from a long bout with cancer. They were looking for communication and closure with their daughter, who clearly came through and affirmed her presence with memories of her childhood and appreciation for the things her parents had done for her. After we closed our communication, their other daughter shared a story about glimpsing Sarah's passing at the very time it occurred.

Sarah had been staying in her childhood room. Her sister had a dream that the room transitioned into a fairytale scene with a bed fit for a queen, lavish dressings, and a huge canopy. She saw her ill sister being held by Jesus. He appeared as Sarah's teenage ideal of Jesus: a "hippie Christ" with a headband and colored robe. As Jesus held Sarah in his arms, He made her feel very warm and comfortable and seemed to be flirting with her. She had a big smile on her face.

The next morning, the healthy daughter woke to find that Sarah had passed away during the night. As she told this story, my heart was filled, knowing that she had been fortunate to glimpse her sister passing into the arms of her beloved during the dream.

While we may not all experience a glimpse behind the veil between this world and the next, we can rest assured that our loved ones are greeted by family and friends on the other side. We can help them cross over more peacefully by allowing them to express what they feel, hear, and see before and during the process of crossing over.

I often visit people in the hospital who are quite aware that they are close to death. During this time, they begin to speak of visitors who come and go from the other side. It is not uncommon for loved ones who have already passed to communicate as these patients start to cross over and get in touch with the other side. Those who have passed are letting the patient know that family, friends, and loved ones are waiting for them. Whether in this world or in the spirit world, we are never really alone. We only need to accept the presence of love in our hearts and, through this connection with Source, there is comfort and peace. Love is far beyond our human comprehension, and, in that love, we are cradled in the arms of Creator and connected to all living things.

Sometimes the process of crossing over makes other people in the room uncomfortable. They make statements about the patients losing his or her mind or "talking out of his head." You hear people say, "He keeps saying he's seeing people." Or, "It must be the drugs they're pumping into him."

Often, as a medium, I hear and see other spirits around the person who is crossing over. They are letting go of their life on earth and beginning to communicate with long lost family members whom they are about to join. It is only fear that prevents us from sharing this true message.

Many years ago, a dear friend of mine learned that his father had terminal cancer. I was able to spend a good deal of time with him during his last few days on earth. Toward the end, he took my hand and said, "I am about to go on an incredible journey!"

I was amazed— not because of his plans for the afterlife, but because he had always professed to be an atheist. He was so pleased about the journey awaiting him.

I encourage you to listen with the ears of your heart to your loved ones. Let them know that you are aware that they are about to embark on a great journey. Make sure that you do not tell them or anyone else they are talking out of their heads. If you observe and listen, you will share in a transition from this world to the next. Draw on your inner strength to guide you and to remember: Love never dies. Birth as well as death is a Sacred journey. Sharing your loved one's leaving the earth is an opportunity for you to experience the final moments of your loved one's life on this planet.

Benefits of Ceremony

It is no accident that funeral ceremonies have been performed for thousands of years. Ceremony brings peace to both the living and the dead as souls transition into a different state of consciousness. Whether you offer a simple prayer, or participate in a basic funeral or an elaborate celebration, ceremony helps all of us let go and begin to heal.

There is always great sadness in losing those we love, and we must allow ourselves space to grieve and accept a new phase. We must also offer gentle guidance and peace to the loved ones who leave to help them through the transition. Taking time to share feelings of love and joy and even jokes or funny memories makes our love grow deeper and allows the healing to begin.

My mentor and friend, Dr. Michael DeMaria, a three-time Grammy Award nominee, uses music to help people through transition. Voice, flutes, percussion, and other musical sounds soothe the soul during the dying process and help those crossing over to find their way home. This is the process he shared with me in a personal interview.

> *"Cross-culturally, music has often been used to help ferry souls to the other-world after shedding the mortal clay body. I have used the flute many times working with family, friends, and hospice. I'm always amazed at the power of sound to help during a transition that so often brings up emotions too big for words. In some cultures, people spend their whole lives learning their death song to help them have a good death. Song helps make the transition with an open heart and mind to welcome the dying process as a crowning achievement of living well."*

Knowing that a loved one has passed or is soon to pass takes us to a different place. This special knowledge breaks our hearts and yet it opens us. We should be willing to surrender with the realization that we have no control over the situation. Though we are challenged emotionally and mentally, we can also share in a very special gift of love by helping our friend or family member feel truly loved and appreciated as they cross over. Great healing can take place when we keep our hearts open and allow ourselves to be in touch with our emotions. Love can be shared with only a smile and unimaginable healing can take place when few words are required. Love never dies; it only continues.

I have been to funeral services where a selection of the favorite songs of the deceased was played. It is wonderful for the attendees to enjoy the music and it helps them remember and think of those who have passed in a gentle and fulfilling way. When the soul/spirit of the departed is attending the service, they also enjoy this music.

Ceremony 7.1: A Practical Suggestion for Musical Ceremony

Select or let your loved one select a beautiful piece of music. Offer to play the music for them when they are close to passing. Let the music soothe them and aid them in their passing. By all means, if you are a musician and are able to play the requested music, offer your wonderful gift. This ceremony may also be used during the time of a cremation or burial to assist the soul in crossing over.

As a medium, I know that sending love and understanding to someone after death is always beneficial. I recently acted as a medium for an older gentleman, nearly eighty, whose daughter had passed only six years before. As she appeared and I described her, he confirmed it was she. I began to relay the things that saddened her about decisions she had made during her life like taking drugs and surrounding herself with people who were not good for her. She knew she had become mixed up in some bad things. As I was telling him this, he started to cry. At that moment, her demeanor changed as well. She smiled and lightened.

I could feel her love. His tears truly lifted her. She said that she was able to move on after witnessing his tears.

We must allow ourselves time to grieve and to be sad. Our tears come from the heart and can help heal us. They seem to wash us clean. These tears can also help release our loved ones. In the end, the gentleman was elated and relieved that his daughter had been able to share with him and that in some way he had touched her and helped her through his love.

When we leave this world, we also leave behind everyone and everything we have come to know on this planet. We are carried by universal energy from this world to the next. Whether you sing, dance, cry, or laugh, honoring death as a rite of passage provides peace and support as our loved ones go through the transition.

Ceremony 7.2: Saying Good-bye to the Departed

Join your family in a circle. Place a candle and photo of your loved one in the center. You may also add a crystal or adored object of the person in the center of the circle. Allow each person time to speak from the heart about the person who passed. Say a prayer and ask for the peaceful crossing of your loved one. Send them blessings for their journey and let them know that you want them to be at peace.

My son's very good friend lost his mother (we'll call her Terry) when she was in her late forties. I attended the funeral. I could see Terry watching the service, looking very pleased at the turn out. The priest even mentioned that it was incredible how many people were there, particularly on a Monday morning.

After the service we followed the procession to the cemetery, which was in the country and very quiet and peaceful. Terry's gravesite was near a large oak tree. As the service ended and the minister began the final prayer and blessing, a mockingbird began to sing from the tree. When the mockingbird finished his song, I saw an angel take Terry in his arms and ascend. She had a big smile on her face and she was ready to depart.

I hugged her son and said, "You know I talk to spirits." He said, "yes." I then shared with him what I had witnessed, and he tearfully nodded in acceptance.

Believe it or not, most people's spirits/souls are present at their ceremony or funeral. They usually wait until the body is lowered into the ground, cremated, or disposed of in some other fitting fashion before crossing over. Funerals are great for noticing whether the spirit is still present or will soon after be on its way. Our awareness, respect, acknowledgement, and love during this time helps spirits cross over.

Most of us, given the opportunity, would be surrounded by loved ones and have the chance to say good-bye to family and friends before death comes to visit. Unfortunately, we seldom know how or when we will take our last breath. When a loved one passes, especially suddenly, their spiritual consciousness may remain in a state of shock. Our simple guidance can help them realize what has happened so they can come to terms with it and peacefully move on. Here is a ceremony to help your loved one see that it is time to move on.

Ceremony 7.3: Helping the Departed Recognize Their Passing

Light a white candle. Place the obituary beside the candle so the person who passed can read it. Or write down the name, time of birth, cause of death, and time of death of the person who passed. Speak to the spirit and gently let them know that they are no longer able to

return to the human body. The spirit can read the letter
illuminated by the candle to help them realize what has
happened. After recognizing their death, the departed
may leave the earth plane in the arms of their angel.

I did this ceremony following my father's sudden passing. He had a heart attack and died while visiting my brother; this was quite unexpected—for us and for my father. Consequently, the suddenness of my father's passing created a need—a need for him to become fully aware of his own death. During the ceremony, I felt him leaning over my shoulder to read the note. I sensed his taking it all in and almost instantly coming to an acceptance. I felt relieved and I knew that he did as well. Whether you feel a presence or not, this ceremony gives the departed a chance to understand the situation and what they need to do next.

Death is a rite of passage, which should be accompanied by honor and respect by letting ourselves grieve and by sending love and peace to the soul that is taking its journey. It is easy to get wrapped up in the hustle and bustle of funeral arrangements and push grief to the back burner. But, tears, consciously shed, heal the heart and keep the door of love open. People do leave in the arms of their angels. I have witnessed it many times.

Opening Your Awareness

My first memory of talking to and seeing someone who had passed occurred when I was five years old. I was at the funeral of my Aunt Annie, who was quite elderly when she passed. I remember almost sitting in my mom's lap, kind of leaning onto her and looking around the church. There were flowers. It was a sunny day. The church pew that we were sitting on was hard and about half full of people. I looked up in the balcony and there I saw Aunt Annie watching her own funeral. She looked quite happy to see all the people and flowers.

My mom was crying and I leaned over to tell her the good news: "Aunt Annie's here Mom; she's in the balcony watching; she's okay." My mother told me to stop talking and continued to cry. Undaunted, I felt pretty good about Aunt Annie's looking so happy.

I can assure you that, after having had communication and confirmation with hundreds of people who have lost loved ones, the departed can hear us. They miss us and they sometimes have regrets and unfinished emotional business. And, at times, they visit and want to communicate with us as much as we want to communicate with them. A medium simply acts as a receiver for the spirit to come through.

Being a medium certainly can be demanding at times, but my work also brings me great joy. Imagine how it feels to witness the love and peace, which often comes with many tears, to the person left behind when they realize their loved one is alive and well in spirit form!

One of my favorite experiences with love and the afterlife occurred when a woman (we'll call her Linda) came to me hoping to learn more about communicating with the love of her life who had passed after a long illness. They had met when they were both retired and well into their sixties. They fell madly in love with each other—sharing intense feelings that neither had ever experienced before. Sadly, after only a few years together, Linda's true love passed.

Linda shared with me that one day, almost four years after his death, she found herself unable to stop crying. The tears continued off and on all that day and she could not understand why. She could not stop thinking about her husband and felt that he was with her in spirit. She wondered if this sudden onset of powerful emotion might be linked to the anniversary of the day that he had proposed to her. She, however, was not certain of the exact date.

That night, Linda decided to go into the basement and look through some of her husband's possessions that she had stored after his death. Perhaps she could find some clue if not an answer. She entered the basement and the first item that she found was her husband's day planner. She opened the planner to the same date, several years earlier. There, in his writing, were these words: " Linda said Yes!"

She knew at that moment, without a doubt, that her departed true love had guided her to his day planner. What a joy for her to know his love for her was still so very real and that he most definitely was communicating with her from the other side.

Another similar highly emotional experience took place when a young man visited me whose wife (we'll call her Denise) had passed away while they were traveling. They had been visiting orphanages and adoption agencies in a foreign country and the conditions were difficult. They were sad and disappointed with the trip because they could not find a child that they felt was right for them.

The day before they planned to return home, Denise insisted on going to one more place. Her husband was not up for the trip so she went without him. The weather took a turn for the worse after she left. During her drive to the orphanage, she drove into an icy stretch of the road and tragically lost her life in a car accident.

David felt incredibly sad and guilty for years because he had not accompanied Denise on that last visit. At the time that he made an appointment with me, he had never before visited a medium or psychic, but wanted to know how the accident happened. As I connected with Denise, she showed me enough images of the accident to provide David with a better understanding of how it unfolded. She showed me that she was in a remote area when the weather suddenly changed. She lost control of the car on the ice and lost consciousness almost immediately after the crash, without suffering.

Spirits will give enough information to confirm their presence to another person by providing details of the causes of their death, memories of the past, or something that resonates with the person seeking advice. Confirmation comes before information—which may be new to the seeker—is revealed. In this case, David's wife confirmed her presence with many details to help him believe.

David had been extremely depressed during the two years since Denise had passed. But now she was sending him love and telling him to go out and meet people, live his life, and be happy. Several months later, I was delighted to hear that David had met someone very special and was enjoying a new relationship.

The spirit world is infinite; there is no jealousy or ego on the other side. Our loved ones wish for us to continue on with our lives and find all the happiness we can. Talking to those who have crossed over and listening to their regrets as well as all that they love has truly helped me and those people with whom I have worked to realize how precious life is.

When a dear friend of mine lost her son in his early thirties, her family suffered great heartbreak. Her son had been tragically killed by another person. And then, only a year after his death, her home was almost destroyed by a hurricane and most of her most important personal possessions were lost. On Mother's Day, months after the storm, a neighbor came to her door with a silver baby cup. Engraved on the cup was the name of her son and his birthday. She recognized this to be the same little cup her son had drunk from as a child. The neighbor had been scuba diving not far away and had found the cup in the sand. My friend came to realize that her son was letting her know how very much he loved her. After all, the day that the cup was returned was Mother's Day!

Some people ask me if I feel that my memories of another world help me in an intuitive sense. It may, in fact, be easier for me to access my intuition in this world because my past lives are so ingrained in my memories.

Our past can help or hinder our ability to interact with the spirit world. On the planet I remember being from, telepathy is as natural as speech; loving intention is practiced for healing purposes as well as being a normal component of general behavior. It was natural and "normal" to speak to creatures of the sky or planet with our thoughts. We were able to communicate with incredible accuracy without cell phones or any other type of device. We were aware of our connection to each other and the essence of life that flows through all living things. All creatures were respected and honored.

We were also telekinetic, which gave us the ability to easily move objects with our minds and freely travel through thought or time—from one place to another. I also remember a flying craft that we would use to go long distances to other planets. We ate vegetable and mineral matter; eating meat was not something we considered. There was a harvesting of something like seaweed from the water and it contained many nutrients.

Crossing over was greeted with gentle ceremony. Communication with the other side was common and shared with family and community. We held ceremonies asking the spirit to be free and to assure us that all who were left behind would be well. We believed that, after death, the body became a part of the environment again. The body became soil, flowers, plants, and trees; and new life was born.

So for me, it feels natural when spirits speak to me. I never really questioned it or thought it was strange. But, I did grow up understanding that people on this planet often found these things unusual or even unacceptable. Most of the time, I kept my communication with the other side to myself. There were very few people who I chose to share this information with, but I understand now that when we are afraid to listen or be open to new ideas, it is only because we are not ready. Fortunately, I had great support from my grandmothers and from my parents—all of whom were very intuitive.

Whether my stories of another world resonate with you or not, I hope that you can keep an open mind about these things, for there are many others with memories of other worlds. For example, General George Patton often spoke of past lives, memories, and battles, and he let it be known that his information and experience from past lives assisted him in many of his battle plans. One may ask why he remembered. Perhaps it was because he was ready to remember and ready to apply the lessons.

Many people similarly want to know how to communicate with the other side and feel that they are not able to do so. Even as an experienced medium, I have had to confront occasional doubts. During a reading I once did for a group, one of the family members, who only spoke Spanish, came through. I did not completely understand the message. But, I passed along the words the best I could. The family understood and that was what mattered.

When we communicate with ancestors, guides, or loved ones from the other side, we must recognize that we are equally alive, still part of the same infinite field of consciousness. The difference is our loved ones are no longer in human form. It is important that we take the time to feel the pain and sadness of our loss. Tears help us heal our heart and eventually find peace. We have no control over losing the ones we love, but we must each work with ourselves to find a way through the process of grieving. Communication or connection to your inner spirit and heart will assure you of finding the answers to help you along the way.

Many times as a medium, I have had the opportunity to communicate with people—friends, sons, daughters, fathers, mothers —who sadly took their own lives. They have much work to do on the other side and go through deep regrets and sadness. Sometimes they get "stuck" until they feel forgiven or simply feel loved by those loved ones who have been left behind.

Suicide is possibly the most difficult way to lose someone, but they need our attention and love after death, as much as we need theirs. Often, during my communications with those who have perished by their own hands, they share how they felt prior to taking their lives and they relate how they were unable to see a way out of their pain or addiction or seemingly hopeless situation.

Fortunately, I have had the honor and the joy of witnessing many departed souls find peace with their loved ones and accept their end on earth. After they find closure, they greet their angels who joyfully carry them from a place between the worlds to the other side. Each of us has a guardian angel who loves and stands by us . If we are unwilling to accept their presence during this life, we can be certain that we will find them waiting for us with open arms when we cross over.

Letting Go of Suicide

We must remember; love never dies. I have never heard any spirit tell their loved ones or me that they regretted not leaving more money in the bank. I have never heard anyone in the spirit world complain because they did not get a promotion or the car they always dreamed of. What I have heard repeatedly is that they regretted not spending more time with children or a spouse or that they have regretted the way they treated their loved ones. They have shared the sorrow of not knowing how to reveal the love in their hearts while they were on Earth, yet they freely shared their love from the other side.

As I stated previously through working as a medium, I have been honored to assist in helping many lost souls cross over after taking their own lives, and it has been a joy to share communication from the deceased to many people left behind. It is helping others to find this incredibly important closure and peace—the knowledge that their loved ones have gone on and are now in the light—that may be the most rewarding, fulfilling part of my work.

I once worked with a good friend of mine who told me that the father of her granddaughter's child had recently taken his own life. I offered to speak over the phone with her granddaughter (we'll call her Jessica) and share any communication that I could with her.

I was able to establish contact with the young man (we'll call him John), and Jessica told me that she was receptive to his presence. John shared with her his new knowledge of the pain and sadness, which he had caused her and their beautiful child.

John had an addictive personality and had been unhappy for years. He was unable to accept the beauty and love that his life had offered him. He was unable to complete his mission on earth and chose to end his life with a gun. He related his reasoning for taking his life so sadly and violently and that he realized obviously too late that his act of desperation was a terrible mistake. John let Jessica know that he would have committed suicide no matter what she had done because of his own blindness. He cried as he shared his love with her. She opened her heart and cried as she told him of all the love she felt and continued to feel for him.

I began to see John's angel approach him from behind. The young man's head had been turned down in sadness during the contact that we had been having with him. The more Jessica shared her love, however, the more John became able and willing to raise his head. Finally he saw the radiant angel standing behind him. He turned and the angel carried him away. Jessica's love freed John to leave the earth plane. This was love without blame or guilt; it was acceptance.

I simply lit a candle for John as we spoke and let him know that he was free to leave. I could not help crying myself. Later, Jessica wrote me a letter thanking me for sharing my gift with her. I still treasure her letter.

Ceremony 7.4: Ceremony to Assist the Soul Who Committed Suicide

Any loving persons who wishes to assist this individual cross over may be present during this ceremony.

Light a candle in the center of your group, or in front of yourself. It is helpful to have more than one person because more individuals can send that much more love and acceptance. You may add flowers or incense to create a sacred space.

Speak to the deceased as if they are in the area of the candle. Speak the name of the deceased and the cause of death. Listen and focus on what you feel.

Let the deceased express any feelings of sadness or regret; simply listen and respond with love.

Tell the deceased: "You are free to leave now and go into Creator's arms. Your angel is waiting to guide you."

Allow yourself to imagine an angel. If you are clairvoyant, watch for the angel. As the angel approaches the deceased, the energy begins to change. Your love and light help facilitate the change.

As the deceased recognizes the love and presence of their angel, they realize that they are loved and will accept what they have done. You will feel the deceased depart. You may see the departure or hear a sound of confirmation or simply feel the release.

Say a prayer for the departed. You have helped set them free.

Ceremony allows us to transition into new awareness. In the case of the passing of a loved one, the new awareness embraces the concept that the departed remain equally alive, still part of the same field of consciousness. The difference is that our loved ones are no longer in human form. Communication or connection to your inner spirit and heart will assure you of finding the answers to help you accept the loss of your loved one.

Try to listen to the departed spirit and do not let ego get involved or start analyzing the experience. Give yourself permission to make mistakes. It does not matter if the message is not 100% accurate. What matters is that you feel the presence and the love of the departed spirit.

I believe that with practice most people can communicate with the other side. Each and every one of us is born with a sixth sense: Our intuition is always available to guide us. All we have to do is ask. As you open the door to possibilities, your sixth sense will take you to rich unexplored places that you may journey to as you choose. The more you trust your inner guidance, the more quickly you are able to access it. Sometimes you must simply act upon your intuition and the results will amaze you. We all must learn to recognize the difference between our own ego and intuition and, consequently, to sense when we need to let the intuition take charge.

It is the world of the ego that attempts to persuade us that things we experience through intuition are untrue. Our culture is just beginning to recognize how we create through thought and how energy can heal. These were a part of ancient cultures but in the times of fast-paced technology, we have convinced ourselves all to often that we do not possess this intuitive power. But, yes, of course we all do. We simply need to practice feeling good, listening to our bodies, and learning to develop this inner trait.

You do not have to remember past lives or other worlds to begin accessing your intuition. You can start with a few minutes of sitting in silence while focusing on nothing but your breathing. As you also open yourself to communicating with those who have passed, remember that a response does not always come immediately. Sometimes simply offering to listen helps you to become receptive enough to hear, to know when you both are ready.

Ceremony 7.5: Messages From the Other Side

Pick a time and place that feel right to you. You do not need a lot of time, but plan for at least twenty minutes. Try to practice around the same time each day to start recognizing signs of communication. Take some deep breaths, focusing on your breathing and your body as your breath. Start with a declaration:

> *"I am open and receptive to all love and abundance in the universe."*
> *Then state the name of your loved one:*

> *"[NAME], I am open and receptive to any messages that you, my loved one, have for me."*

> *You can listen to soft music, pray, and speak your feelings or write them down. During the ceremony, you can ask questions, send love, or simply tell the departed that you are ready to accept messages from him or her.*

> *You may perform this ceremony as a free-form practice of meditation or select a guided meditation which allows you space after a certain point to simply sit. Often such meditation helps us to relax and quiet the mind without much effort. As you repeat this practice, you will find yourself receiving answers....*

Be still and listen. You may be surprised at the results. For example, after you have prepared by completing the previously described ceremony, you might turn on the radio and hear your loved one's favorite song (on two different stations!). Or you may hear a song that was very special to you and your departed loved—a song that you had not heard in years. This is your answer!

Similarly, you may turn on the television and it just happens that the favorite program of your departed loved one is on. Perhaps a lamp will flicker or your television or some other appliance will turn on and off. You may smell a certain fragrance or scent of the person. Yes, they are talking to you! One of my clients always recognized her grandmother's White Shoulders perfume when she came into her room late at night.

As you continue this practice, you are connecting with the spirit of your loved one and opening the door for more to come through. The contact that you may be seeking may or may not occur during the time frame that you have chosen. Your practice lets your loved one know that you are open and receptive to their love and any message they might have for you. Try to go with it and trust your feelings and your imagination. If you think something that you feel, see, or hear is your imagination – set aside your resistance and trust what you are sensing. What you are experiencing can very likely be the spirit's way of communicating with and talking to you.

Listen to your heart and reap the gifts of the love that fills us all. We all have capability to talk to spirits as well as accessing many of our lifetimes. We each must make an effort to have a practice. Whether it is yoga, meditation, shamanism, or regularly attending church or temple, consistency is the key.

All too often, children come into the world being told that spirits or angels they may speak of when they are little are simply figments of their imagination. They are taught to shut down a natural connection with the intuitive parts of themselves. This is very sad because we all have intuitive abilities, which should be nurtured and encouraged. As we become adults, it is important to work with ourSelves to regain inner awareness through meditation, prayer, and a willingness to be open to awareness.

When I was a child, my father and grandmothers were wonderful about confirming my sense of spirit. My grandmother often spoke to me of dreams and visions and talking with angels. I am incredibly thankful for this upbringing. Yet, I am keenly aware that, as strong as my intuitive Self is, working with awareness is a life long process that must not be neglected.

I urge you to pray and meditate with your children and grandchildren. Teach them about the roots of your ethnic background and that each culture has spirituality which goes back into the roots of our ancestry. When we grow up with awareness of a higher power, we learn to respect others and ourselves and, in turn, everything on our beautiful planet Earth. The only way our world will become sustainable and peaceful is through awareness now and in the future.

We cannot tell how long the gift of being human will keep us on this planet. Beyond the Earth, there are many other planets and dimensions—all with purpose. The beauty and truth in you connects you to all living things in the entire universe. We must take responsibility for bringing good and kind intention into each ceremony. There is never reason for anything but kindness and love. Let sacred ceremony and ritual become directly integrated into shift you into all that you dream, and, in your dreams, expect miracles. May you have a sweet and sacred journey, live in peace, laugh often, and love with all of your heart.

Conclusion

"All I know of Spirit is this love." – Rumi (translated by Coleman Barks)

Ceremony and ritual have been a part of human existence since the beginning of time. Our very being contains seeds and imprints of ceremonies from lifetimes before and it is our sacred responsibility to keep ceremony alive for future generations. As The Native Americans say, "the Earth is both our Mother and our Grandmother" and that our spiritual practice will reach the next seven generations. We must honor and respect Mother Earth, for without her, we would not be here. Incorporate thankfulness to Gaia as part of your ritual. The beauty and truth in you connects us all and brings joy. We must take responsibility for bringing good and kind intentions into all ceremony and ritual that we practice. There is never a reason for anything but kindness and love. Let sacred ceremony and rituals shift you into all that you dream of. May you have a sweet and sacred journey, live, laugh and love.

Resources

Michael DeMaria, Ph.D., *Ever Flowing On*, 2001

Living Buddha Living Christ, Thich Nhat Hanh
Riverhead Books, 1995

Alberto Villoldo, Ph.D., *Illumination*
The Shaman's Way of Healing, 2010 Hay House Publishing

Alberto Villoldo, Ph.D., *Shaman, Healer, Sage*
2000 Harmony Books, NY, NY

Anam Cara, John O' Donohue
Cliff Street Books, An Imprint of Harper Collins 1997

Depak Chopra, The Seven Spiritual Laws of Success: A Practical Guide to
the Fulfillment of Your Dreams, Amber Allen Publishing, 1994

Hanna Kroeger, *God Helps Those Who Help Themselves*, 1984
Hanna Kroeger, *The Seven Spiritual Causes of Ill Health* 1997

Of Water And The Spirit, Malidoma Patrice Some
Penguin Compass, 1994